THE POWER AT THE BOTTOM
OF THE WELL

THE POWER AT THE

Transactional

BOTTOM OF THE WELL

Analysis and Religious Experience

MURIEL JAMES
LOUIS M. SAVARY

A COLLINS ASSOCIATES BOOK

HARPER & ROW, PUBLISHERS
New York, Evanston, San Francisco, London

Library of Congress Cataloging in Publication Data

James, Muriel.
    The power at the bottom of the well.

    "A Collins Associates book."
    Includes bibliographical references.
    1. Experience (Religion)   2.   Transactional analysis.
I. Savary, Louis M., joint author.   II.   Title.
BL53.J35 1974   200'.19   74-4639
ISBN 0-06-064115-0
ISBN 0-06-064116-9 (pbk.)

FIRST EDITION

CONTENTS

v

PREFACE

We're excited about this book, and we hope you'll also find it exciting. We wrote it for people who, like us, are searching for ways to clarify their religious experiences. Although everyone has a variety of religious experiences, we discovered that few possess a psychological frame of reference for evaluating them. Transactional Analysis has proved to be such a tool for us. And we'd like to share what we found.

A previous book, *Born to Love: Transactional Analysis in the Church,* was written to help understand the dynamics between people in a local church, learning to relate in dialogue. *The Power at the Bottom of the Well* expands Transactional Analysis concepts to wider perspectives of religious experiences and deals with the problem of setting free the benevolent spiritual energies within people, so that they might enjoy more fully the religious experience of knowing their own OKness.

In particular, we show how people's ego states—the Parent, Adult, and Child parts of their personalities—may influence their theological ideas as well as their transcendent religious experiences.

Incidentally, we've used all of our ego states in writing this book.

From the Child in us comes our excitement, joy, enthusiasm, and a feeling of being OK with each other, with you, and with God.

From the rational Adult in us comes information and techniques to use in self-understanding.

From the Nurturing Parent in us comes the biblical proclamation restated in contemporary words, "God says you're OK."

MURIEL JAMES, M.Div., Ed.D.   LOUIS M. SAVARY, S.J., Ph.D.
Lafayette, California   South Belmar, New Jersey

1

IS THERE ANY WORD
FROM THE LORD?

Jer. 37:17

An Introduction to Transactional Analysis

WHERE IT ALL BEGINS

Deep in everyone lie the questions, Who am I? Why am I? Where am I going? and How can I *be* with all those other people?

Who am I? Well, I'm just Jane or John Doe going about the business of living. Sometimes I do it well, sometimes I'm pretty mediocre, and sometimes I actually mess up things. And I feel not-OK.

And I wonder, *why* am I? And why am I, *I?* Why *am* I here? What's it all about?

Then once in a while the sun suddenly comes out and lights up a field of cowslips, or a pile of new-mown hay, or a clump of tall trees bending in the wind, or bubbles of white water foaming over rocks. Or I see the look in someone's eyes turned to me in anguish or joy, with pleading or a desire to share. Then I know. Just for a fleeting moment, I know I am who I am, and I know why. And I feel OK.

And then the moment passes, and I wonder, *Where* am I going? What's it all about? Are the moments of flowers and bubbles really real, while the daily grind is somehow less than real? Or is it just the reverse? Because if either is true, then how can I *be real?*

How can I *be real* with all those people, not just *do* things with them?

And once in a while I pick up a Bible, and I look for the passages of hope; and I find some, and I wonder, Could it possibly be true that God says I'm OK? And once in a while, from deep within, a sense of being affirmed wells up, and I believe, at least for the moment, that it just might be true. I just might be OK with God.

Is there any word from the Lord?

Recently, looking for some "word" from the Lord, I attended a coffee hour where people of various faiths were discussing their beliefs. I felt confused by some of their statements. "The Bible is the most inspirational book I ever read." ... "Whenever I begin reading the Bible in bed, it puts me to sleep." ... "I feel that Jesus wants us to be gentle and show kindness to each other." ... "Jesus was a revolutionary; so what are we doing sitting piously here in our little church?" ... "The pastor knows best; so we should obey him." ... "Our pastor doesn't know what it's all about." ... "We've been trying to change our worship service for years!" ... "We want our mass to stay the way it's always been." ... "You can't trust people who go to church." ... "I just love it when we sing 'Faith of Our Fathers.'" ... "I don't think our new pastor even believes in hell." ... "Of course, I believe in miracles." ... "Of course, I don't." ... "All children should go to church school." ... "We'd have a better world if our teenagers dated only those with similar beliefs." ...

Sometimes after meetings like that I don't know what I think! I often find it very hard to know what is the word of the Lord and what isn't.

Some comments seem to contradict others, for example, the inspirational Bible that becomes a sleep-inducer, and the meek and mild Jesus also seen as a social reformer. Contradiction is not unusual, I know. Conflicting ideas and misunderstandings often occur among people in the context of religion.

Some people search for ways to deal with such problems, and some people avoid them.

A PSYCHOLOGICAL TOOL

This book presents Transactional Analysis (TA) as a psychological tool for understanding different responses that different people make to religious experience. It won't avoid ideas that are sometimes in conflict. Frequently, differences of opinion, apparently theological, will be seen in the light of psychology to be rather heavily influenced by personality differences. For example, by those who have a negative self-image, God's love may be viewed as punishing and repressive, while those who are happily in tune with life often experience God's love as comforting and liberating. Chapters attempt to show how theological and psychological elements can be understood in ways that help the reader think more clearly and act more effectively in daily life and in religious life.

Transactional Analysis, a well-respected and well-accepted psychology, was developed by psychiatrist Eric Berne, M.D. Originally used by professional psychotherapists to help mentally ill people understand themselves, TA theory and method was found to be so practical that people in families, in schools, in business and industry, in religious organizations, and in all the mental health fields soon discovered new ways of applying its techniques. People began using TA to understand themselves, to enhance their relationships with other people, to deepen their relationship with God, and to expand their religious experiences.

In this regard, Transactional Analysis has five distinct advantages over most traditional psychologies like those of Freud, Jung, Adler, Sullivan, and others.

FIVE ADVANTAGES

First, *TA is a self-help psychology.* While most approaches involve counselors, clinicians, psychologists, therapists, psychiatrists, and other professionals, TA theory can have a startling effect on people

simply when they read about it. Its basic concepts provoke immediate responses.

Certain psychological problems involving religion that can be dealt
with outside the counselor's office are frequently clarified with the
help of TA. Of course, TA is not only a self-help psychology; many
professionals employ its concepts with patients in therapy. In minutes, people versed in TA theory can often explain its basic ideas to
others. Young people from age seven can grasp TA concepts and use
them quite capably.

Second, *TA is a nonthreatening psychology.* While many theories delve
into unconscious cellars of the psyche and preoccupy themselves
with sexuality, selfishness, death drives, primal traumas, and other
subsurface problem areas, TA deals with easily observable behaviors
—ordinary conversation, smiles, frowns, gestures, and other forms
of body communication. Religious problems that emerge clearly in
everyday behavior and conversation are often quite apt for TA
analysis.

Third, *TA is a psychology of change and personal enrichment.* Some
traditional psychologies intend only to help people conform or to
behave the way others expect them to behave, not to change or
grow. TA is designed to help people change for the better. It is a
psychology filled with hope. No matter how they view themselves
—whether drowning in a negative self-image or buoyed up by a
happy sense of self—people can use TA to increase self-awareness
and open up areas for growth, especially in self-worth and relating
to others. TA can help people caught in the current of religious
change discover many ways to enhance their approach to God and
religious experience.

Fourth, *TA is immediately effective.* Troubled people often spend long
periods with religious counselors and psychotherapists before they
uncover their problems and begin to search for solutions. With TA,
after only a short time—sometimes in minutes—people begin to
have insights about themselves, their needs, and the ways they can
change. Learning TA can immediately affect the quality of a person's

religious response. People already familiar with TA can learn to nurture their own religious growth as well as that of others.

Fifth, *TA is a psychology for mentally healthy people.* Most psychologies have been developed by therapists for dealing with emotionally disturbed persons or to use in crisis situations. Since people don't have to be sick to get better, TA asserts that even healthy people can learn to feel more secure in their OKness and more freely responsive in their relations with others. TA proves especially helpful in developing trust, growth, love, and hope.

People are very complex. Religious experience and reactions only serve to complicate people more. In this regard, TA's ability to simplify things points out another advantage it holds over other more complicated theories. TA may not be *the* word from the Lord, but it can help clarify the word; and that's a useful, exciting, joyful experience.

THE PERSONALITY

People often ask, How come I acted the way I did? or How come you acted the way you did? Every human personality, explains Dr. Eric Berne, seems to have three distinguishable ego states. Each is a unique system of feelings and behavior. Berne calls these systems Parent, Adult, and Child (P-A-C). At any moment in time, people can function from Parent, Adult, or Child ego state or sometimes from two or three ego states simultaneously.

Berne's P-A-C terms have special meanings which will be discussed in the following sections. The words *Parent, Adult,* and *Child,* when capitalized in this book, refer to ego states, not to actual parents, adults, or children.

THE PARENT EGO STATE

Humans learn how to be parents from their own parents. Mothers and fathers serve as models for their children, creating, for better or worse, an emotional climate that fosters growth or hinders it. The Parent ego state develops in children as they record and incorporate attitudes and behaviors of their mothers and fathers. If grandparents, older brothers and sisters, housekeepers, or other grown-ups significant to them, play a parent role, the Parent ego state may also record them. All significant parent figures experienced in childhood combine to make up our Parent ego state.

According to TA theory, the Parent ego state is like a videotape in the brain that contains laws, admonitions, and rules about thinking, feeling, and behaving that we heard from our mothers, fathers, and other grown-ups. These tapes also include all the things we saw them do and the ways they did them.

Among these Parent tapes are the hundreds of *verbal* dos and don'ts, the yeses and nos that were directed at us such as, "Don't talk back," "No candy between meals," "Get down on your knees when you pray," "Remember the starving . . . and clean up your plate," "Always brush your teeth after meals."

Mottoes like the following often found their way into our Parent ego state during childhood years: "Look before you leap." "A stitch in time saves nine." "Don't cry over spilt milk." "Big boys don't cry." "If at first you don't succeed, try, try again." "Waste not, want not." "Never trust a stranger." We never evaluated these rules or mottoes as good or bad; we simply incorporated them from the authority figures we were expected to please and obey. We incorporated both the specific words and the admonitions beneath the words.

Other admonitions, both positive and negative, came *nonverbally* through tone of voice, the cuddling and cooing, the scowls or smiles, the tender or hurtful touch that told what was pleasing and what was not.

Later on, people become parents to their own children or act like parents to their friends, younger brothers and sisters, and begin to use the same clichés. They may even speak in an authoritarian manner as though they now had *the* word from the Lord that previously their parent figures seemed to have.

Certain familiar physical clues reveal the Parent in action: furrowed brows, worried looks, nagging index fingers, scowls, patting on the back, foot-tapping, consoling touch, and many others. The Parent often uses sentences sprinkled with *always* and *never* and *once and for all.* The Parent tone of voice may be condescending and punitive or supportive and sympathetic. It can be recognized by its abrupt judgmental expressions such as "Silly!" "Naughty!" "Shocking!" or its unthinking responses such as "How dare you?" or "Not again!" or "This is the last time I'm going to tell you!" or "Let me do it for you." Each of us has some special Parent words, opinions, and gestures that are uniquely ours.

Sometimes there are conflicting Parent rules inside us. For example, "Treat people fairly" conflicts with "Don't let people get in your way." Or one part of the Parent in our head may say, "When you pray, use the words 'forgive us our *trespasses,*' " while another part may say, "The proper expression is 'forgive us our *debtors.*' "

In our Parent we include the rules we incorporated, without evaluating, from many parent sources. Naturally, some Parent tapes may conflict with others. Conflicts usually reflect the contrary ways of thinking and behaving we witnessed in our mother and father, who at different times acted in their Parent, Adult, or Child.

Since mothers and fathers also have P-A-C ego states, children will incorporate aspects from each of their mother's and father's ego states. This includes whatever mother and father copied from *their* parents. It includes their Adult abilities to think and act rationally; it also includes the sense of freedom or lack of it and the specific adaptations or lack of them that were in their parent figures' Child ego states. Children reared by substitute parents will incorporate elements from the ego states of the substitute parents. Consequently, conflicting Parent statements inside us are not surprising.

The Parent can be a great help to the personality so that ordinary habitual things we do—brushing teeth, combing hair, washing our face—can be carried on efficiently. These activities and hundreds like them are performed routinely according to rules and procedures internalized in the Parent, providing useful dos and don'ts meant to protect children and assure survival.

On the other hand, Parent-dominated personalities can be a burden, especially if such people feel compelled to do things exactly "the way they've always been done" or to make others conform to their rules. The person who is a Constant Parent may, for a while, elicit a compliant obedient Child from others, but eventually others withdraw or respond from their rebellious Child.

People with a strong Parent often appear to others as domineering, self-righteous, or as having all the answers. They like to moralize about everything and couch their advice in verbs like *should, ought,* and *must.* While the Parent can be positive and helpful when nurturing, it can also be harmful, negative, and punishing when oversolicitous.

Strong Parent personalities are legion in religious institutions, among church authorities, and wherever doctrines, dogmas, commandments, rules, and regulations are formulated and enforced. Religious people who operate primarily from the Parent ego state often treat others as if they were children. They may come on as saintly people who like to take care of everyone's problems; they may come on as authorities who know all the answers; they may come on as benevolent dictators collecting people around them who are willing to be dependent and subordinate.

People who recognize their own Constant Parent[1] and want to change can learn to do so. First, find the people, places, and situations that tend to trigger your Constant Parent; second, take note of your own Parent statements and recordings, and examine them; and third, begin to change them, revise them, or create new ones.

Take a Moment

Write down the names of two important parent figures you had when you were little. Under each name list several things they did that you liked and several things they did that you didn't like *when you were little.*

After your list is complete, ask yourself if you ever do any of those same things and if so, with whom. Whenever you do, you're acting from your Parent ego state.

THE CHILD EGO STATE

In TA the Child ego state does not mean little person. Like the Parent, it is a set of recordings in the brain collected from the earliest age. While the Parent recorded observable external events—what grown-ups said and did—the Child recorded inner responses and conditioned behavior learned in childhood. Your Child ego state is the child you once were.

Uncensored, natural feelings, learned and conditioned feelings of hurt or happiness, curiosity or fright, loneliness or closeness—all shape the Child part of the personality. These inner feelings of the Child are often outwardly expressed along with laughter, tears, quivering lips, temper tantrums, and the like.

Whenever feelings dominate reason, the Child probably holds sway over the personality. Magazine advertisements often are designed to appeal to the reader's fun-loving Child, greedy Child, sexy Child. For example, many ads are contrived to elicit sexual feelings. A particular perfume may be described as *the* ideal way for a woman to attract a man. Shaving lotion ads may communicate to men a similar sexy Child message.

While many feelings in the Child are positive, negative feelings also abound. Physically, very young people see themselves as small, clumsy, dependent. As tots they are helpless to do effectively many things they see others do easily: speaking properly, using a fork, reading a book, and so on. Moreover, signs of disapproval from mothers and fathers bring on feelings of being rejected and discouraged. When infants feel urges to explore closets and private drawers, to tear paper and bang spoons, some grown-ups demand they give up these satisfactions. Prohibitions usually generate more negative feelings. In TA, these are called "not-OK feelings." For some children, the very situation of childhood—having to wait a few minutes for a clean diaper or waking up alone at night in a dark room

—produces these negative experiences, making the Child in them feel "not-OK."

The Child's positive emotional experiences lead to what Berne calls "OK feelings." Touching a cuddly animal, chewing on an apple, and having someone love us are usually joyful experiences for the Child in us. Whenever we react impulsively and say "Wow!" or "Great-o," that's a positive Child response. So is laughter, dancing, jumping, smiling, giggling, clapping hands, shouting for joy. It is the Child in us that can be loving, warm, and affectionate, also curious, imaginative, and creative. The Child likes to daydream; it imagines doing great things and saying great things.

Some favorite Child expressions include "I want" and "I wish" and superlatives like "biggest," "fastest," "strongest," "best," and so on. The Child can cleverly avoid grown-up responsibilities with expressions such as "I can't," "I don't know" or "I don't care." The Child seeks signs of approval and often does things to get compliments.

According to TA theory, the Child is made up of three parts: the *Natural Child,* the *Little Professor,* and the *Adapted Child.*

The *Natural Child* is that part of the Child ego state that is the untrained, uncensored, and expressive infant. Self-centered, capable of violence as well as closeness, the Natural Child is not concerned with good or bad but with what it impulsively desires. It prefers pleasure over pain, responds immediately to bodily feelings, loves to fantasize, and is incessantly curious. The Natural Child is what a baby would be naturally if nothing influenced him or her to be otherwise. The Natural Child responds to religious experiences of desire, joy, movement, enthusiasm, love, and mystery. Rhythm and melody, colors and scent, are strong activators of this part of the personality.

The *Little Professor* is the emerging Adult in the Child, the unschooled wisdom of the Child, the part that is intuitive, manipulative, and creative, that plays hunches and can read nonverbal messages. The Little Professor intuits in others the good as well as the evil and responds to religious experiences that stimulate intuitive and creative talents.

The *Adapted Child* develops in response to the experiences and parental training that influence and modify the Natural Child's inclinations. Adaptation (or conditioning) begins immediately after birth. Infants learn to adapt to outside authority, for example, eat on schedule or tolerate a wet diaper, because of the need to survive and the need for approval. From interaction with parents and their environment, the Adapted Child in children develops a sense of right and wrong. Other adaptations in the Child ego state may include obedience to, or rebellion against, laws and commandments, the development or lack of development of conscience and ethics. Sometimes children respond to religious experience characterized by fear, threat of pain or separation, and rebellion, and sometimes to religious experience characterized by love and encouragement.

Because the Child is the part of the personality that allows people to be emotional, spontaneous, outgoing—to touch and feel and experience people and things—the Child enriches many religious experiences, especially those which express inner emotions, such as celebrations (weddings, baptisms, first communions), holidays (Christmas, Easter, Thanksgiving), and prayer experiences in which the feeling is personal and spontaneous.

While the Child can express delight, enthusiasm, charm, and spontaneous positive feelings, it is also capable of taking over the entire personality—by being overly aggressive and assertive (stubborn, resentful, never satisfied) or regressive and submissive (colorless, retiring, sullen).

People can learn to keep from being hooked into their Child without diminishing its enthusiasm, or, if they do get hooked, they can learn to get unhooked. The unhooking process involves becoming aware of Child responses that tend to dominate the personality. Learning to hold back impulsive reactions by counting ten gives the Adult a chance to evaluate the Child response and to modify it if necessary.

Take a Moment

Go to a quiet place. Get comfortable and think back to when you were a child. See yourself as a little boy or girl in a situation where you really wanted something very much.

After recalling the childhood situation, ask yourself which part or parts of your Child ego state were most involved. Your Natural Child who wants what it wants when it wants it and aggressively gets it? Your Little Professor who intuits, creates, and manipulates to get what it wants? Your Adapted Child who was trained to say or do specific things to get what it wants?

THE ADULT EGO STATE

In TA theory the Adult ego state means something quite different from being a grown-up since even little children possess an Adult ego state. The Adult is characterized by actions based on rational thinking. Whenever people act in reasonable ways, we say they are acting in their Adult.

Following a thinking approach to life, the Adult analyzes pieces of facts, information, and experience, much the way a computer processes data. Also, like a computer, the Adult operates in the personality by finding facts, testing reality, seeing possibilities and alternatives, and making decisions. Whenever people are remembering, questioning, classifying, clarifying, inspecting, interpreting, evaluating, planning, verifying, or choosing, we say their Adult is in command.

The Adult may be distinguished from Parent and Child. While the Parent responds automatically, stating traditional rules and regulations, the Adult is that part of the personality whose responses tend to be rational and well thought out, showing the ability to decide for oneself a reasonable way to act. On the other hand, while the Child may frequently cry or need help in getting out of an awkward situation, the Adult inspects the situation and calculates ways to get out of it.

In general, while the Parent deals in rules, and the Child focuses upon feelings and behavior in response to rules, the Adult handles facts and decisions.

Adult behavior may be identified by a concern for information and facts. The Adult often asks, Who? What? Why? Where? When? and How much?—not as a Parent might in order to be judgmental, or as a Child might to harbor resentful feelings, but to help clarify things for himself or herself, as well as for others.

An important Adult function is to coordinate the ways the personality expresses itself. Coordination involves testing Parent data to see if it is still reliable ("Do I really look terrible in green clothes? Someone told me I did, ten years ago.") and gauging Child responses to make them appropriate to the situation ("It's alright to cry now. People will understand."). People feel secure and OK when most of their Parent data is reliable and holds up under testing ("I can count on my Parent."), and they can let their Child responses come out knowing that they will match the situation ("I can count on my Child.").

As people learn to coordinate their personalities from the Adult, they realize that the Adult can permit spontaneous responses from the Child and Parent without losing control.

The more completely people are in touch with their Child and Parent recordings, the more easily they can separate Child and Parent responses from Adult ones. The more sensitive a person is to his Parent and Child, the stronger and more autonomous become Adult responses.

Take a Moment

Recall the past week. Remember a decision you made.

Was it a decision your parents would have approved of (Parent)? Did you make a decision on the basis of your feelings

(Child)? Or did you gather facts and think about them before you decided (Adult)?

INTEGRATING THE PERSONALITY

Those new to TA might be tempted to conclude, "Parent and Child responses are bad and unproductive; I want to respond always in the Adult." This is a distorted viewpoint. People who are always perfectly reasonable (Constant Adult), so much so that they show no emotion (locked-up Child) or never do nurturing things for other people (locked-up Parent), do not present attractive, well-balanced personalities, More desirable is a happy mixture of Parent, Child, and Adult—with the Adult in the driver's seat.

Well-balanced personalities in leadership roles seem to have three essential qualities that make them effective. They display *justice* (a Parent quality), are open to *fun and humor* (a Child quality), and strive for *competence* (an Adult quality).[2] A successful organization, be it a family, a church, or a business, will usually possess these same three characteristics.

Healthy people blend all three ego states into harmonious and unique formulas so that they are not overly emotional (Constant Child), or too judgmental and punishing (Constant Parent), or exclusively colorless and computerlike (Constant Adult). The well-balanced and mature person—what Erich Fromm calls the fully developed person and Abraham Maslow calls the self-actualizing person—can be sensitive, creative, and loving (Free Child), efficient, protective, and caring (Nurturing Parent), as well as reasonable, reflective, and self-controlled (Adult).

People in the process of personal integration, says Berne, learn to take responsibility for everything they feel, think, and believe. They show three kinds of tendencies: *personal attractiveness and responsiveness* (integration of Child), *ethical responsibility* (integration of Parent), and *objective data-processing* (maintaining primary Adult functions).

Under Adult control, expressions of Child feelings and Parent rules can be genuine, well-integrated, personal responses to actual situations. For example, angry temper tantrums may point up a rebellious Child, but legitimate indignation or outrage *based on Adult observation* of actual injustice usually indicates responsible and well-integrated behavior.

In a similar way, enforcement of arbitrary or irrelevant commands may signal a punishing Parent, but actions motivated by ethical principles developed in the *light of Adult scrutiny* probably indicate a well-integrated person. In his Sermon on the Mount, Jesus' new commands are an example of authentic ethical principles.

TA AND A WORD FROM THE LORD

You may be wondering about our enthusiasm over TA. You may be wondering if we think of it as *the* Word. No, we really don't. It is *a* word but not *the* Word. But, since Transactional Analysis vocabulary helps explain people's personalities, how people transact with each other, and what they can do to enhance both, we do think that the Word may be heard more clearly and religious experience deepened through the process of learning TA.

One person wrote:

Before Berne—the church was where I went to gain some measure of hope and courage for life. But quite often I came away feeling dissatisfied with myself and sensing that maybe there really was no hope for me since I wasn't and couldn't be perfect.

After Berne—what a difference! Now I realize that my Child ego went to church. The church, as a parent figure, was making me aware of how bad I was and reminded me of the wrongdoings rather than encouraging the potential for good.

My Child was, and is, afraid to express views contrary to what it thinks are the church's views. But my Adult has a greater sense of responsibility. It should express its opinions on what it sees as right and wrong about the present church and help bring about beneficial changes.

My relationship to the church is becoming more meaningful and rewarding. I am eager to find out how to think for myself theologically, not just accept what others tell me. This is involving study, but it's very exciting.[3]

The fact that you've started to read this book indicates your interest in religious experience. You may claim not to understand religious experience; you may sometimes even doubt people are capable of it. But deep within, you know there is such a thing. And you find yourself looking for it.

You may have searched for the Word in the Bible, may have listened for the Word in church, may have looked for the Word on some disguised Emmaus road. You may have done it deliberately, or with partial awareness, or without any awareness. But it seems to be part of the nature of people to search for ultimate truth, for the meaning and reason for existence.

Each ego state is unique; each has different responses; therefore each may hear a word from the Lord in different ways.

Take a Moment

Let your mind relax. (If you let the muscles around your lips smooth out and your eyelids hang loose, if you let your tongue "float" on the air in your mouth, you are likely to find your mind beginning to float.) Let your mind wander through your collected memories until you come to a time when you hoped to hear the Word or needed to hear the Word or feared to hear the Word. Go back to that experience. It is there within you and can be replayed as if it were on videotape. See yourself again in that particular situation. Let yourself reexperience the pain or the joy of it. Don't think about it; just *be* in it once more for a few minutes.

Now consider what part of your personality seemed to be involved. Was it your Child ego state, perhaps, feeling excitement and gladness, laughter and joy, fear and guilt? Was it your Parent ego state, perhaps, acting critically and punitive, nurturing and loving, or indifferent and bored? Was it your Adult ego state, gathering information, analyzing the situation, making rational decisions?

Which ego state or states were most involved in the memory replay of your search for religious experience?

2

DO YOU KNOW THAT GOD'S SPIRIT DWELLS IN YOU?

1 Cor. 3:16

The Inner Core and the Power Within

A DEEPER LOOK

Where do people find the *energy* to be kind and loving? Why do some people usually seem smiling, eager, and ready to go, while others seem to be tired, hesitant, or ready to fly off the handle?

Where do people find the *vitality* to develop close relationships? Why is it that some people without trying can listen understandingly and attentively to others and make friends easily, while some people frequently friendless, become quickly impatient with others and intolerant?

Where do people find the *drive* to be creative, to study, to work? Why can some people apply themselves for hours on end, while others can't seem to concentrate and often give up before things get done?

Where do people find the *strength* to believe in God and to accept the challenges of faith? How is it that some people seem to be strong believers, almost unshakable in their faith, while others are weak and doubting?

Some people seem to have boundless energy—to love, to trust, to encourage, to work and study, and to believe—while others seem quickly to run out of steam. Why do some people seem to have all the power they need, and others, hardly any?

Perhaps it is necessary to look more deeply within people—beneath Parent, Adult, and Child—to find a source for their strength and power. Is there an energy that unifies the three ego states? Is there some inner strength—a power within the self—that certain people seem to possess, which others lack?

THE INNER CORE

A recently developed TA concept helps account for the flow of energy in people's personalities. We like to call it a person's *Inner Core.* This concept was introduced in *Born to Love* under the name "spiritual self."[1]

The spiritual self or Inner Core is not the same as Eric Berne's "self." Berne's "self" in TA theory refers in general to the ego state a person is freely expressing at any particular moment. The spiritual self or Inner Core refers to what people call their deepest self, the real me; it is somehow independent of the three ego states.

While Berne's "self" can continually change from Child to Adult to Parent, the Inner Core is seen as a *permanent personal reality that underlies all three ego states.*[2]

From another point of view, the Inner Core corresponds to *me as self-programmer* of the P-A-C tapes that I consciously play in daily life. The Inner Core can program expressions of its ego states much as a driver of an auto can steer his vehicle in the directions he wishes and at the speeds he wishes.[3]

Independent of the ego states, the Inner Core interpenetrates and channels energy to all three of them. Like a coffeepot stem that allows steam to rise upward to brew the coffee, the Inner Core allows energy to flow throughout the personality and shape it. Parent, Adult, and Child ego states provide three expressive outlets for Inner Core energies.

Every beautiful red apple began originally as seeds of energy within a tender core. The fully grown apple was shaped through its core. Captivated by the apple's color, shape, and aroma, we easily forget the importance of its core. In a similar way, people can become overly involved in expressive ego states and forget the Inner Core.

From the Inner Core comes motivating force to change personality. For example, the Inner Core is influential in radical re-Parenting; that is, in developing new and effective Parent tapes, as well as in implementing new natural and creative Child tapes or in transforming a Constant Adult.[4] Although the Adult ego state may design and oversee new tape making, the Inner Core helps explain why some people seem to have the power to improve themselves, while others don't. All ego states can be transformed when the Inner Core chooses to call upon the power present within it.

"Power is the birthright of every human being," wrote Rollo May. "It is the source of his self-esteem and the root of his conviction that he is interpersonally significant."[5]

When people's Inner Core seems blocked or finds distorted expression, symptoms appear which include despair, fear, destructiveness, violence, and many others. Rollo May labels the disease *impotence.* Though violence at first glance might seem to be the opposite of powerlessness, impotence is precisely the root disease. Impotence describes a conviction that I am less than human and unwelcome in the world. In this situation, the Inner Core's usual expression— positive, hopeful, and interpersonal—has somehow been blocked, distorted, or damaged. As a result, it erupts violently and sometimes despairingly. Rollo May called the Inner Core's disease impotence, "fully recognizing that violence also requires for its triggering some promise, a despair combined with the hope that conditions cannot but be bettered by one's own pain or death."[6]

Take a Moment

Let your memory go to some time in your life when you felt helpless or hopeless and therefore impotent. Then imagine a movie screen in front of you showing a film of that situation. Watch what you do; look at your facial expression and body posture; listen to your words and tone of voice. Observe your impotency. Next, look at a different movie, one that shows you as feeling confident and acting competent. Watch what you do; look at your facial expression and body posture; listen to your words and tone of voice. Observe your potency. Compare your Inner Core in the two situations.

THE POWER WITHIN

The energy channeled to the three ego states by the Inner Core is a positive personal force—a power for good and growth. We term this force the Power Within. Others may prefer to call the source of this inner power God, Spirit, Nature, Ground of Being, or some other name. Paul the apostle was referring to the Power Within when he asked, "Do you know that God's Spirit dwells in you?"[7] To describe the Power Within, Jesus used the water-of-life symbol. "If anyone thirsts," he said, "let him come to me and drink. As Scripture says, from within him will flow rivers of living water."[8]

The idea of the Power Within permeates Judeo-Christian tradition. The Bible often associates inner power with God's Spirit. "I am filled with power," shouted the prophet Micah, "with the Spirit of the Lord, and with justice and might."[9] "God did not give us a spirit of timidity," explained Paul the apostle, "but a spirit of power and love and self-control."[10] Jesus gave those who believed in him the Power Within.[11] "You shall receive power when the Holy Spirit has come upon you," said Jesus.[12]

People never need to run out of this inner power since its source is the divine power creatively pulsing deep down within everything in the universe. A loving God, maintaining contact with each living

FIGURE 1   21

THE INNER CORE

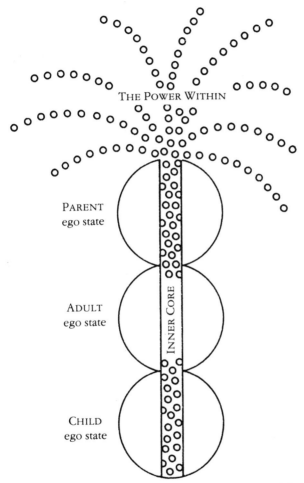

Parent, Adult, and Child ego states are all penetrated by a single
Inner Core, referred to as "the spiritual self" in *Born to Love*. The
Power Within (symbolized by the moving dots), acting through the
Inner Core, affects all levels of the personality.

thing and energizing it from within, seems continually to pour life-energy into people's Inner Core. The Inner Core, in turn, gives expression to this inner power through Parent, Adult, and Child ego states.

According to TA theory, everyone has the ability to grow healthier and live more fully. Jesus assured his followers that his Father would never cease to desire and actively work for the fullest loving transformation of each individual. We feel that the energy or strength for such growth flows through the Inner Core, finding its ultimate source in the Power Within—"the rivers of living water." The Inner Core can allow the Power Within to be released, thereby enriching and strengthening the personality. The Power Within also springs forth to help create relationships of intimacy with others and with God.

CREATING RELATIONSHIPS

According to TA theory, people have the ability to relate to others in loving, trusting ways. Such positive relating describes the fundamental idea in the life-stance toward others called "I'm OK—You're OK."

Many people, however, are frequently involved in destructive transactions of one kind or another, such as those described in Eric Berne's book *Games People Play.*

Where do people caught up in such destructive games find the courage and strength to stop playing them and begin establishing healthy and loving relationships with others? What enables people to initiate and nourish what Martin Buber calls "I-Thou" relationships?

In such relationships, people are called upon to give of themselves. What motivates people to give of their inmost self? To extend their own identity without forfeiting it, in order to create a relationship? Whence comes the desire and the thrust to encounter people on this "I-Thou" level?

Here again, we feel, the source of motivation and energy for building genuine relationships is the divine power acting through the Inner Core. Eric Butterworth describes this power as "the divinity within."

In all human relations it is good to begin with the principle that people are innately wonderful and beautiful—and *love-full.* It may be hard to see, for they may not see it in themselves. But people are real even beyond their superficiality. With practice, you will find that you can look through them instead of just at them. You will salute the divinity within them and celebrate love as the one great reality in which you both live and move and have being.[13]

Everyone's Power Within ultimately has the same divine source. Because people enjoy the Power Within in common, they share, at their deepest levels, a connection with each other and together feel a oneness, a communion of love and trust.

Like branches belonging to the same vine, people are connected to each other by a shared inner power. Source of life and energy, the vine sends its life into all the branches. Those open to the Power Within are ultimately all interconnected in life and love. The choice to be open to this loving Power Within belongs to each Inner Core.

The strength and resources for forming "I-thou" relationships with others and with God are already flowing within each human. As Jesus expressed it, "I am in my Father, and you in me, and I in you."[14] The Power Within allows people to love powerfully.

In the Inner Core, divine power is made incarnate in people. Many, however, seem unwilling to discover it, almost afraid. It seems that if they were to get in touch with the love-energy available in their deepest selves, they might have to live up to it. And, undoubtedly, this Power Within calls for a response.

Its discovery, like finding the secret of life, is an inner experience— a conversion, not merely the acquisition of new information. It may happen at the very time when a person feels most disheartened, and often occurs in unpredictable ways.

Some may have read many books, heard many sermons, accumulated much knowledge of science and art, with the hope of some significant idea or thought bursting through to transform them. But frequently it is a rather insignificant happening which strikes them—a word, an encounter, a death, a recovery, a look, or a natural event. God uses such experiences to reach people—whatever will put the Inner Core in touch with the Power Within.

THE CLOSED AND OPEN SELF

Cynthia is often the life of the party; she's great as a mother, but hardly the best person to send to the university library on a research-gathering task. In TA language, Cynthia's life-of-the-party quality indicates an open flow of energy from her Inner Core to her Free Child; her mothering capacity indicates a free flow to her Nurturing Parent; while her fact-finding weakness may indicate a partially blocked energy-flow to her Adult.

Fred, on the other hand, usually acts quite ethically (strong Adult), but displays very little love and warmth toward others (closed-off Child). People like Fred may never experience intimacy because they find it impossible to share with another person their deepest feelings.

In relation to the three ego states, the Inner Core may be (1) *open,* (2) *closed,* or (3) simply *out of touch.*

If energy flows freely from the Inner Core to one or other ego state, we may describe the channels as *open.* An open person is characterized by trusting and loving acceptance of others.

If the Inner Core is open to the Parent, people will tend to express toward others positive caring and nurturing qualities found in the best of mothers and fathers.

If the Inner Core is open to the Adult, people will learn to make decisions on the basis of facts, but also on the basis of other people's feelings and well-being. Decisions, usually open to influence from surroundings, will be made to help preserve the total environment rather than to exploit it. The Power Within helps the Adult generate responsibility for the decisions it makes.

Influence of an Inner Core open to the Child will often express itself toward others in attractive childlike qualities such as affection, warmth, curiosity, and playfulness. Loving feelings tend to permeate these relationships. Some people discover that they can pick up, as if on an inner radar screen, the feelings or vibes of others in a room. This is one talent of the intuitive Little Professor; from time to time people in touch with their curious and intuitive Child may say to another, "I'm picking up from you that you're feeling sad (or happy, or anxious, etc.). Is that true?"

When energy-flow from the Inner Core is blocked from one or other ego state, we may speak of the channels as *closed.* Closed persons are characteristically shut off from others. Appearing rigid, anxious, frustrated, and the like, they often operate in isolation rather than in relation (either to other people or to God). Energy remains bottled up, unexpressed. Inner power is like health—we tend to be unaware of it until we experience its absence.

Sometimes, people are closed only in one ego state while open in others. For example, the Power Within may permeate the Child but not the Parent; such people at times may be affectionate (strong Child) in their relationships but unwilling to set reasonable limits on their behavior (weak Adult); or they may be curious (strong Child) yet irresponsible (weak Adult); again, they may be warm and playful (strong Child) but are unable to see when others are hurt, or discouraged, or have special needs (weak Parent).

Sometimes energy flows freely from the Inner Core into the Parent, but not into the Child. In this situation are people who care for other people's needs (strong Parent) but often without warmth (weak Child); people who are usually dependable and nurturing (strong Parent) but seldom show feeling and affection (weak Child); people who are tradition-keepers (strong Parent) but without enjoying it (weak Child), for example, people who arrange the annual office party but don't know how to delight in it.

In other cases, energy permeates the Adult but is blocked from the Parent and Child. Here are found executives who make rational decisions (strong Adult) yet are insensitive to needs and feelings of their employees (weak Parent), and people who are consistently reasonable and rational (strong Adult) but lack the curiosity and enthusiasm (weak Child) that could make for truly exciting living.

Ideally, there can be open channels between the Inner Core and all three ego states, so that an individual's self-expression would be nurturing and caring (Parent), warm, affectionate, and curious (Child), as well as responsible, rational, and ready to make personal decisions for the benefit of many people (Adult).

While some people seal off their Inner Core and others keep it open, still others are *simply out of touch* with the Inner Core and its energy. The Power Within is there already, only it is unperceived. And hence people do not use it to express themselves. Perhaps some believe that no such power is readily available to them and consequently do not count upon it. They seem like rich old men who prefer to believe themselves poor rather than to open their inner rooms and count the fortunes sitting there.

Some people may claim, for example, they have no Child ego state. TA theory would say that everyone has a Child ego state, but that in this case the Child is either closed off, unused, or forgotten.

Channels from the ego states to the Inner Core seem to need to be activated or else they tend to become closed off and weakened. People can learn to let the Power Within vivify their Inner Core and energize Parent, Adult, and Child ego states.

Eric Berne makes the analogy: "If no radio is heard in someone's house, that does not mean he lacks one; he may have a good one, but it needs to be turned on and warmed up before it can be heard clearly."[15]

The Child seems to be the best ego state with which to begin the process of getting in touch. Learning to relax is a good exercise. Simply enjoy the feeling of being at rest. Let *enjoyment* of happy and satisfying experiences, like feeling relaxed, become a habit. Enjoyed experiences need not be special or unusual, but can be simply little things—like the ability to breathe, a friendly smile, a glass of water, a beam of sunshine, and the like. Practice enjoying these happenings, and soon the channel from Inner Core to Child will begin to open to the Power Within.

SIN AND THE POWER WITHIN

In their deepest selves, says TA theory, people are OK, agreeing with the biblical "God saw that it was good" view of creation. Those who make vital contact with their Inner Core will discover this fundamental OKness. Theologically, this is a first step in religious growth, for it enables believers to put off the conviction that they are ineradicably sinful and destined to be NOT-OK forever.

People sin when on purpose their Inner Core selfishly attempts to hold up the stream of things and events on their way to God, that is, when the Inner Core consciously blocks the natural outgoing flow of the Power Within. Self-centeredness makes sin destructive and unnatural. Yet even sin seems not to be able to thwart the working of the Power Within.

"Every time we mention Original Sin," writes biblical theologian Alan Richardson, "we ought also to mention Original Righteousness."[16] In other words, although we all tend to put ourselves in the place of God by setting ourselves at the center of the universe (Original Sin), there is another equally fundamental side to human nature where the vestiges of the divine image and power remain in us (Original Righteousness). For example, we *recognize* our self-centeredness and realize that it is an inadequate response to life; we also know that our deepest needs are for community, for reconciliation, for intimacy relationships with other people and with God.

In one sense, this book is about Original Righteousness: how it may be recognized in the Power Within transforming the Inner Core and expressing itself in the personality through the Parent, Adult, and Child ego states.

A fundamental premise is that beneath all the human self-centered pride and sinfulness, beneath all the psychological garbage accumulated in layers of hate, jealousy, anger, anxiety, resentment, envy, lust, and the rest, there "at the bottom of the well" lies a core of goodness.

"To feel half dead when life calls is a tragedy. To feel angry for being born is heartbreaking. To feel dismayed or hopeless when the sun rises or sets is a waste of the *Love* that was given 'in the beginning.' "[17]

RELIGIOUS EXPERIENCE

Religious experience may be described, psychologically, as awareness of the Power Within penetrating the Inner Core, flowing through Parent, Adult, and Child, and expressing itself in a relationship to God. TA theory offers a way to observe the growth of such a relationship. For example, if the Power Within flows through the Child, the relationship with God will tend to be warm, affectionate, and trusting. If it flows through the Parent, the relationship will probably emphasize the nurturing of others and caring for their needs. If it flows also through the Adult, the relationship will usually feature reflective themes of wisdom and truth, responsible decisions, and the like.

When the relationship toward God takes a negative turn, TA theory also suggests ways of diagnosing the problem psychologically.

For example, when the Power Within is blocked from the Parent, certain destructive capacities will begin to surface in behavior that is intolerant of others, condescending, dominating, devouring, over-nurturing, prejudiced, belittling (not clever, but bludgeoning).

When the Power Within is blocked from the Child, destructive behaviors begin to be expressed in loneliness, guilt, anxiety, fear, extreme laziness, rejection of others, overaggressiveness, the need to be perfect, consuming lust, violence, and many others.

Adult destructive capacities tend to show themselves in insults (with intent to wound), being closed to new ideas, disregard of others, belittling (snide and "clever"), a sense of superiority, selective fact-gathering (to distort the true situation), selfish decisions, failure or refusal to decide.

Some people's symptoms will indicate being out of touch with the Power Within. In them, so far as the inner demand for religious experience is concerned, the Power Within is absent. Perhaps in some, the need or desire for God has never been clarified or cultivated. Others may have found that their childhood religion offered sufficient comfort, and, lacking outside pressure, they continue to maintain an essentially juvenile formulation of religious experience —one that avoids a mature response to the Power Within.[18]

Take a Moment

Right now, get in a comfortable position, preferably in a quiet place. Allow yourself to grow calm. Let your body feel as though it were sinking into the chair, the bed, the floor, the grass—wherever you are resting. Then imagine that from the top of your head to the bottoms of your feet, there is a core— like an apple core. Imagine this core pulsating with warmth, excitement, and joy. Experience it from the top of your head to the bottoms of your feet. Let the pulsing increase until you experience it moving down to the tips of your fingers. Now imagine the tips of your fingers open, so that all the tension, anxiety, grief, frustration, unhappiness, and so forth drains out. Let these feelings really drain out; let them be pushed out by the force of the joy and excitement and warmth pulsing within you. When you feel drained of the unpleasant feelings, imagine the tips of your fingers closing again, but keep experiencing the pulsing beat within. Experience the fresh potency, the fresh calmness, the fresh Power Within.

THE POWERS WITHOUT

When people refuse (or seem unable) to relate openly and with trust, it may be a sign that the Power Within is not flowing freely. It may also signify that outside forces are exerting negative influences on them. We all seem to act as links on an infinitely ramifying chain of reactions and events.

Everyone has been around people who seem to exude an odor of decay, whose words and behavior belie a flame of brutality or the coldness of despair. Many people, vulnerable to such negative influences, will need to learn how they can shield themselves from them.

Perhaps less brutally but just as effectively, ordinary people can and do pass on their negative responses to others who unwittingly come within their sphere, and these others pass them on to still others, and so on.

On the other hand, everyone has been around people who generate a warm and trusting atmosphere, whose words and actions make others feel free and good and glad to be alive.

The powers that influence people from without may be either malevolent or benevolent. Believers might list devils, evil spirits, corrupt people, and so on, among the malevolent, and count angels, saints, good people, and the like, among the benevolent.

Just as people can learn to recognize evil influences and avoid them, they can also learn to recognize positive influences and seek their presence.

A person out of touch with the Power Within, which is always benevolent, will usually be much more susceptible to malevolent influences from the outside. Laura Huxley writes,

The behavior of the worried, upset or unhappy person reacts on those around him, sometimes more destructively than an infectious disease. Most infectious diseases, such as measles or flu, are self-terminating after two or three weeks; whereas the neurosis, born of a bad experience, not only can last a lifetime, but can form a powerful and subtle chain reaction that goes on and on and is extremely difficult to stop.[19]

Unable to mobilize the energizing Power Within, such people's Parent, Child, and Adult ego states are more likely to respond helplessly or unthinkingly to outside influences. Like trees that bend to any wind that blows, out-of-touch people will appear happy and loving when the outside influences are happy and loving, anxious and mistrusting when outside influences stress fear and mistrust, and so on. In each case, personal responses will be momentary and superficial since the responses are not coming through the Inner Core but are effected from outside the person.

In the following chapters of this book, TA concepts are used to suggest psychologically new ways of helping people understand and enhance their religious experience—prayer, fellowship, social action, going to church, reading the Bible, shaping ethical beliefs, getting in touch with God.

Those presently not in touch with the Power Within may learn ways to begin making contact with it and opening channels to their Inner Core. Those who already know that God's Spirit dwells in them and enjoy genuine religious experience may find ways to enrich it and share it with others.

Perhaps everyone will at least discover, through familiarity with TA concepts, some psychological ways to help clarify their religious experience.

The Power Within—the positive, creative, loving, outgoing divine force operating within every Inner Core—affirms in each individual the fundamental message that unspokenly underlies the entire TA theory; the message that enables people to view themselves and others as important, valuable, and worthwhile, "God says you're OK."

Take a Moment

Imagine that you are surrounded by an impenetrable plastic wall. There is plenty of space within the enclosure; so you can move around freely. See this plastic wall surrounding you. Now imagine that outside this wall are some evil spirits or negative influences from others trying to get in. Look at them through the wall. Listen to them. Notice how they cannot get through your shield; you are safe within. When you see how safe you really are, then in your imagination sit down and let the Power Within flow once more. Although nothing can get in through the wall, see if you can send your power out through it. Let your power have a good influence on the negative influences outside the wall. The power at the bottom of your well may be able to transform evil spirits into loving spirits.

3

HOW CAN WE BELIEVE
UNLESS WE HAVE SEEN?

see Rom. 10:14–15

P-A-C Believers

IN THE FRONT PEW

On Sunday the Smith family sat in the front pew listening to Reverend Lancaster instruct his parishioners how they should live their lives. His sermon abounded in terms such as *redemption, righteousness, holiness, salvation,* and *sanctification.*

Confused by these words, young Johnny Smith noticed his father nodding in vigorous agreement with each of the pastor's statements.

Beside him sat Mrs. Smith, smiling whenever Reverend Lancaster said something she liked, looking annoyed whenever he said something that disagreed with her feelings.

Meantime, Johnny wondered, "How can I find out what's true? Do I ask father? Mother?" He asked himself, "Why does Reverend Lancaster use all those hard-to-understand words? What do they have to do with God? How can anyone believe something they haven't seen or heard?"

An individual's ego states may respond differently to religious experiences and beliefs; responses may be in agreement or in conflict. Sometimes the Parent in Johnny asks, "What ought I to believe?" "And what would I like to believe?" inquires his Child. "But what am I able to believe?" asks his Adult.

When Inner Core energy expresses itself predominantly in Parent statements, such believers may be called Parent believers. Reverend Lancaster was often one of these, especially when he directed his parishioners to "do this" or "avoid that."

When Child expressions predominate, persons may be called Child believers; Johnny's highly emotional mother, a Natural Child, responded with her feelings, believing things the minister said only when they made her feel good. Johnny's father, an Adapted Child, swallowed unquestioningly everything Reverend Lancaster said.

Predominant Adult expressions indicate Adult believers; young Johnny's honest questions are a good example of the way an Adult believer's mind functions.

Depending on the Inner Core's openness, every believer displays a unique blend of Parent, Child, and Adult. This blend usually carries over into religious life experience. Various characteristics of Parent believers, Child believers, and Adult believers can be described.

THE PARENT BELIEVER'S RELIGIOUS EXPERIENCE

The concept of religion expressed by Parent believers is primarily based on what they *incorporated* from priests, ministers, Sunday school teachers, mothers, fathers, theology professors, and so forth. For Parent believers, religion is *learned tradition*—it may have happened at mother's knee, on the hard benches at Sunday school, during religion class, behind confessional walls; it may have come from a theological book, a sermon, or the Bible. But the important point is that some authority said it, that it was incorporated into the Parent ego state and repeated to others, generation after generation.

Examples of such statements include the following: "You will go to hell if you commit a mortal sin." "Always remember that God lives in church." "You couldn't possibly understand the writings of St. Paul." "There is only one way to conduct a communion service, and that is the way we do it." "The Bible says to obey the Ten Commandments, and that includes 'Honor your mother and father.' "

When asked what single most important question she would ask God if she had the chance, Betty unhesitatingly replied, "I'd ask him to tell me which parts of the Bible people should believe literally and which parts are metaphors and stories meant only to clarify some point." Betty was asking to be told, "This is what you should believe."

The Parent believer sees religion basically expressed in *rules.* These may take the form of doctrines or dogmas about faith, commandments of the church, directives from a church official, ethical and moral principles, religious traditions, church customs, and so forth. For Parent believers such rules express what it means to be a religious person. Parent believers frequently quote the catechism or the Bible. And they are fond of commands, laws, and sayings such as: "Love your neighbor." "Turn the other cheek." "Bread gained by deceit is sweet to man, but afterwards his mouth will be full of gravel." "No one can serve two masters." "Do not let your left hand know what your right hand is doing." "Seek first his kingdom." Parent believers overflow with rules for living religiously—not suggestions, but rules. They do not offer options or alternatives, but know the "right way" and assert it.

Naturally, then, the focus of religious experience for Parent believers lies in *external stereotyped behavior* toward others and controlling behavior toward one's inner Child. Such people use the Power Within for fulfilling duties, carrying out obligations, performing rituals, attending meetings or church services. For them, going to church on Sunday is important, as well as telling others they must do the same. Parent believers are generally more concerned with externally carrying out the details of a new order, or getting others to do it, than with adopting a new attitude.

Even though Fred doesn't like the new minister, he comes to church because "that's what a good church member is expected to do." He may not enjoy sitting in the third pew and hearing the reverend's sermons, but rain or shine he will be in that pew every Sunday. Fred is in his Child ego state listening to his Parent. He fulfills to the best of his ability all the commandments of God, of the church, of his fellowship group. Rituals may have little meaning for him, but he performs them. It is not for him to question an order given from above; his role is merely to carry out the rules—and to see that others, especially those in his family, observe the rules as well. For Parent-believer Fred, belonging to a church means carrying out the rules of the church.

For hundreds of years many clergy assumed a Parent posture, demanding of their parishioners rote learning and obedience. A 1906 Roman Catholic young lady's guide written from the Parent state illustrated the focus on rules and on the external fulfillment of duties and commandments.

1. You must be careful to say your daily prayers regularly, and never to omit hearing Mass on Sundays and holidays without absolute necessity.
2. You must make it your practice to go to the sacraments at least once every month.
3. You must scrupulously shun everything likely to prove dangerous to purity. You must be on your guard against curiosity, vanity, undue familiarity with young men, improper conversation and immoral books.
4. In confession you must always be conscientious and candid in regard to the sixth and ninth commandments. You must therefore tell your confessor when any suitor for your hand presents himself, as soon, in fact, as you begin "to keep company."
5. In regard to going to dances, or plays of doubtful nature, you must always ask and follow the advice of your spiritual director.
6. You must endeavor always to please your parents and superiors by prompt obedience, a cheerful demeanor, and industry at your work.
7. You must be very cautious in reading novels and worldly periodicals, and content yourself with a small number.
8. You must endeavor very earnestly to live at peace with all men, and for this end you must carefully avoid dissimulation and uncharitableness in word and action.

The Parent believer usually holds onto beliefs with unshakable convictions.

THE CHILD BELIEVER'S RELIGIOUS EXPERIENCE

The concept of religion for Child believers is based on what they were taught in childhood and upon what they *felt inside* when they prayed, went to church, or read religious books. Child believers, like Johnny Smith's mother, blessed with responsive emotions, center on the inner experience of religion—how it feels. They channel the Power Within primarily into feelings. They may remember what their mother taught them about God and how it felt to be there next to her when she talked about God; it was a special feeling, never to be forgotten. Child believers don't usually focus on the meaning of the priest's or minister's words, but on how a sermon makes them feel—good, evil, sorry, joyful, and so on. If Child believers quote a religious regulation, it probably triggers certain feelings in them.

Needless to say, Child believers express religious meaning basically in *feelings and conditioned responses.* For them religion means a series of personal events or experiences that involve feeling responses and are connected with God and good fellowship—in church, at home, in school. "I feel comforted when I read the Bible." "I feel that I'm damned every time I hear Father McLeary give a sermon." "I don't like going to that church." "It was such a beautiful wedding ceremony. I felt God's presence upon the couple." "It would be so easy to study theology if every teacher made you feel as relaxed as Professor Lindsay does."

For Child believers, a sermon or religious book is effective, not because it offers information or an insight, but because it moves them emotionally. For them, religious experience means feeling loved or feeling rejected, feeling happy or feeling sad, feeling guilty or feeling saved. They tend to view the Inner Core as a storehouse of emotional energy. At Eastertime, while Parent believers may be concerned with being at the church on time or sitting and standing at the proper moment, Child believers might tremble with excitement at the thought of celebrating the Resurrection. While an Adapted Child believer might be concerned about knowing the words of the hymn, a Natural Child believer is more likely to be caught up in the joyful emotion of singing and may even completely forget the words.

A recent local church bulletin spoke to the Child in parishioners:

Today is the day for all true spaghetti eaters. Delicious steaming plates of this tasty food will be waiting for you at York Central School from one to five this evening. Service par excellence by St. John's Parish Club members.

Jesus was probably referring to Natural Child believers when he said, "Unless you turn and become like children, you will never enter the kingdom of heaven."[1] He was probably encouraging people to believe the way trusting children do.

Envious of Child believers, many Parent believers wish they could enter feelingly into their own religious experience. When Jesus came to visit the two sisters in Bethany, Martha seemed aware only of her Constant Parent. But, in reality, she was expressing all three ego states at once: applying her skills in the kitchen (Adult), caring for Jesus' needs (Nurturing Parent), and doing what she felt she *should* do (Adapted Child). And with a slightly different emphasis, Mary, though predominantly Adult, was also using all three ego states: making Jesus feel welcome (Nurturing Parent), listening to his ideas and information (Adult), and doing what she wanted to do (Natural Child).

THE ADULT BELIEVER'S RELIGIOUS EXPERIENCE

For Adult believers, the concept of religion is based, not on what they learned (Parent believer) or on what they felt inside (Child believer), but on their own *thinking and reflection.* For them, the Power Within is the power to think. Aware that there are many ways to think about religion and God, Adult believers want to explore the experiences of other believers as well as their own. They discover that a number of theologians may interpret the same biblical passage in different ways.

Adult believers often reflect on their own personal religious experience, try to interpret it, and evaluate it. They may even discuss it with others to see what other minds think.

An Adult believer, George is expected to accept everything his church teaches, but he often asks himself, "What am I capable of believing? How much of what I was taught to believe have I changed through my own imagination and fantasy? And how many beliefs that really aren't relevant anymore has the church handed on out of a sense of tradition? What's really true? How can I believe anything I have not seen?"

Unlike Parent believers who see religion basically expressed in rules, laws, commandments, rituals, doctrines, and dogmas, Adult believers see religion basically expressed in a series of *personal faith decisions*. Rather than simply obey a religious rule or carry out a church directive, Adult believers like to examine a rule, discover its source, and evaluate its importance for themselves here and now.

Sarah is an Adult believer. Usually when she acts, she does so, not because there is a rule, but because she has chosen to act in this way. When the rule and her decision coincide, that's fine with her. But when the rule and her decision differ, she usually chooses to go her own way. While Parent believers may attend church because they are supposed to, Sarah will attend church (if she does so) because she chooses to, because she sees this as the best way of acting in the present situation. For her, going to church is a personal decision.

The Christopher Movement successfully uses an Adult approach, as its founder explains:

The purpose of the Christopher Movement is to encourage millions of individuals to show a personal responsibility in bringing the love and truth of Christ into the mainstream of life . . . the word "Christopher" comes from the Greek term *Christophoros,* meaning "Christ bearer."[2]

Christophers emphasize what one person can do, with the Power Within, to raise the standards of daily life in the community—caring for the sick, feeding the hungry, visiting prisoners, encouraging the disheartened—and to shape the destiny of the world, especially by personally influencing people in government, education, labor relations, literature, and entertainment.

Parent domination, typical of church organizations, is clearly excluded in the Christophers. There are no memberships, no chapters, no meetings, no subscriptions, and no dues. Each individual decides for himself when, where, and how he will use his Power Within. The Christopher motto is "Better to light one candle than to curse the darkness."

Adult believers see religion basically centered in *reflection*. They like to examine and analyze, gather information and meditate upon it. They want to think about what they were taught and what they experienced. After reflection, they may accept what they were taught, modify it, or reject it altogether. They are seldom overwhelmed by feelings or swayed by emotional arguments.

Thomas More, chancellor under Henry VIII, wrote of an imaginary land, *Utopia,* where everyone would be Adult. Its ruler believed that truth would win out in the end.

He especially ordained that it should be lawful for every man to follow the religion of his choice, that each might strive to bring others over to his own, provided that he quietly and modestly supported his own reasons nor bitterly demolished all others if his persuasions were not successful nor used any violence . . . He was certain in thinking it both insolence and folly to demand by violence and threats that all should think to be true what you believe to be true.

Moreover, even if it should be the case that one single religion is true and all the rest are false, he foresaw that, provided the matter was handled reasonably and moderately, truth by its own natural force would finally emerge sooner or later and stand forth conspicuously.[3]

Ideally, because of the Power Within, believers have the ability to blend in themselves a balance of Parent, Adult, and Child believer, so that they can actively participate in church activities and enjoy genuine personal religious feelings.

A summary comparison of P-A-C believers and religious experience is given in figure 2.

FIGURE 2

P-A-C BELIEVERS AND RELIGIOUS EXPERIENCE

BELIEVERS	*Concept of* *religion* *based on*	*See religion* *basically ex-* *pressed in*	*Focus of* *religious* *experience*
PARENT BELIEVERS	What was *incorporated* from parental authorities and others	*Learned tradition,* rules, doctrines, commandments	*External stereotyped* *behavior* toward oth- ers and controlling behavior toward one's inner Child
CHILD BELIEVERS	What was *felt* inside (or wished or imagined or conditioned)	*Internal feelings and* *learned responses* to personal experiences	*Internal events,* feeling holy, sorrowful, etc.
ADULT BELIEVERS	Personal *thinking* about facts, information, and experiences	*Faith decisions* made after reflection	*Reflection,* meditation, study, etc., taking action

Take a Moment

Make a list of five beliefs in your church that you agree with.
Then jot down answers to the following questions:

Are these beliefs ones my parent figures would also have believed?

How do I feel about the beliefs? Joyful, threatened, discouraged, encouraged, relieved?

What information do I have about the truth of these beliefs?

Which of my ego states seem most involved with these beliefs?

LOUDER THAN WORDS

Sooner or later, believers find opportunities to express their beliefs
in deeds. What do believers reveal by their choice of church activity?

Why does Melissa join the choir while Janet prefers to help the church by washing altar linens? What leads Dave to form an adult religious discussion group while Phil feels content to be anchorman on the church's bowling team? What makes Martha start a liturgical committee and Ed begin studies for the diaconate?

Sometimes actions do speak louder than words. Just as believers can be identified as P-A-C by their thoughts, words, and feelings, they can also be recognized by the ways they respond to church activities.

PARENT BELIEVERS AND CHURCH ACTIVITY

The Parent believer's general way of acting in religious matters is *judgmental and nurturing.* Parents are generally concerned with obeying rules and often enforcing them; they are for clarifying what the law says and seeing that others carry it out. Parent believers have a clear set of standards and find rules or regulations to justify every action. They tend to build their lives and activities around such standards, which assume an absolute value for them.

"The church tells us that divorce is evil," Herb told his daughter, "so no matter what happens, you stay married to him, or else." Reluctant to change any iota of the law, Parent believers are often against changes in church regulation, liturgical practice, scriptural interpretation.

Although Carol, a Parent believer, found it difficult to understand how church authority could change its mind and allow drums and guitars in church, eventually she became accustomed to the new regulations; and in a short time she accepted the new way as absolutely as she had the old one. But if changes occur again, and church officials perhaps encourage interpretative dancing around the altar, her Parent will probably express a similar resistance.

Without realizing it, the Parent believer sometimes creates laws where there are none. Luke reports John the Evangelist using a Parent command: "Master, we saw a man casting out demons in your name, and *we forbade him,* because he does not follow with us."[4]

The sense of responsibility found in Parent believers involves *external control* by other Parent authorities. That is, when Parent believers decide to do something—pray, attend religious services, fast, tithe, read the Bible—they usually do it because there is a law that tells them they should do it.

Parent believers tend to carry out unreflectively ethical and traditional church rules; they tend to believe unquestioningly whatever they were taught, primarily because a religious authority has said it. It seldom occurs to them to ask why. Correspondingly, when Parent believers hand on to the next generation their ethical and traditional beliefs, they tell them to do this or believe that because there is a law that says this is the way to act or a doctrine that says this is what we must believe. Confronting Tradition—the way things have always been done—is the theme of the famous show *Fiddler on the Roof.*

Parent believers Frank and Marilyn passed on their own traditional control to the children by making statements to them such as: "Do what the church teaches." "The priest knows best." "Follow the commandments." "Believe whatever is in the Bible." "You must say your prayers every night."

Parent believers are motivated by a sense of *duty.* They view life in general and religious activity in particular as a series of obligations to be fulfilled, chores to be done. They find nothing strange in being motivated by duty in their religious activity because usually their life in general is similarly motivated. They will say, "I do what the church teaches. It tells me what is right and true. And that is my duty."

When Parent believers talk about religion, their speech is characterized by *should, ought, must, always, never,* and similar *absolutizing* words. They are fond of quoting church law, the church officials, the catechism, the Bible, and other authoritative sources.

CHILD BELIEVERS AND CHURCH ACTIVITY

Natural Child believers' general way of acting is *impulsive;* Adapted Child believers' way of acting is *learned;* while Little Professor believers' way of acting is *intuitive* and *creative.*

Corresponding to their feeling-approach to religion and religious experience, Child believers often react in immediate feeling-response to each situation. While Parent believers may do things according to tradition, Child believers frequently do things because the activity provokes good feelings. They like to be carried away by feeling, to be stirred by a sermon, to be caught up in a hymn. Usually for Child believers, the stronger the feeling, the deeper the religious experience.

Like Parent believers, Child believers usually have an unreflective sense of responsibility. In religious matters, as in life in general, Child believers *respond to feeling and conditioning.* While the Adapted Child is trained to do what the law says, Natural Child believers find themselves obeying the dictates of feelings. They often do good to others because of the emotional reward it brings. When behavior is disapproved by grown-ups or authorities, the Child believer usually feels guilty.

Correspondingly, while the Adapted Child believer is motivated by approval and disapproval, the Natural Child believer's motivation springs from *impulse.* "I do what I feel compelled to do in a situation." Often carried by surrounding emotional atmosphere, the Natural Child believer may be energized by good feelings—love, joy, enthusiasm—and debilitated by negative feelings—guilt, rejection, loneliness. For this reason, it is difficult to predict the responses of a Child believer, especially if mind and feelings have recently been infected with a strong emotion. While Parent believers are eminently predictable ("Get Joe on your committee; he'll see that everything gets done."), Child believers change unpredictably ("If Andy's feeling good—but only if he's feeling good—ask him to lead the singing; he'll make the congregation come alive.").

While conversation for Parent believers focuses on "what we must do" or "what is absolutely essential" or "what we have always done in this church," conversation for Child believers usually overflows with emotional statements: "I *really enjoyed* last night's revival." "I *hated* that book; I was *annoyed* reading it." "Why would *anyone* write such a *stupid* sermon?"

The Child believer tends to give identical responses to similar experiences. Psychologically, the Child believer is said to *identify*. If, for example, Jim had a delightful time at his first fellowship meeting, he will expect to have a delightful time at the next one. If the next meeting is emotionally unsatisfying, his disappointment will be greater because of his high expectations. But, because he is a Child believer, he returns to the fellowship meetings, or attends others like them, expecting to feel the same emotional response he felt the first night. Similarly, suppose Pastor Thomas's first sermon annoyed Linda, a Child believer. Then, each time she thinks of Pastor Thomas or comes to one of his sermons, she will probably find herself generating in advance the same feelings (identifying) that she had during his first sermon.

Some Child believers scarred by negative church experiences in childhood—threatened by a priest in the confessional, coerced by a Bible story told in a frightening way, punished for being fidgety in church—will automatically react with those negative feelings in similar situations throughout life: always being frightened at confession, always expecting to be turned off by the Bible, always resistant to attending church.

In his *Note-Books,* Samuel Butler recalls an apocalyptic Child believer's experience brought about by his nurse's comment. "I remember my elder sister and myself asking our nurse if the world might come to an end that afternoon. We were told it might, so we began to scream, and screamed till we were told it mightn't."[5]

ADULT BELIEVERS AND CHURCH ACTIVITY

In contrast to Parent and Child believers, the way of acting characteristic of Adult believers is not judgmental or intuitive but *reasonable*. Adult believers are concerned with figuring out the best way to act here and now. For them there is no absolutely best way to act in all situations. Each time and place offers a number of possible responses, and Adult believers choose to examine the alternatives open to them and to act in ways that are consistent with personal values and shared beliefs. Consequently, Adult believers usually have less difficulty than others accepting change, for example, in doctrinal interpretation or liturgical practice, as long as it seems reasonable and helpful to people. They do not feel obliged to "stick to the way we've always done it" or "the way we were taught." They do not necessarily agree that "if it was good enough for us, it's good enough for our children," though they may, in certain cases.

Unlike Parent believers who are controlled by tradition and Child believers who respond to impulse and feelings, Adult believers are *internally controlled.* They act from within, reasonably and reflectively. Even when they know the appropriate rule or regulation, Adults tend to evaluate the particular situation, so that when they act, whether in line with the rule or against it, they accept the fullest responsibility for their actions. Consequently, when things do not work out, Adult believers seldom excuse themselves saying that they were swayed by feelings (as a Child believer might do) or blame the failure on someone else or on a rule (as a Parent believer might do).

Correspondingly, Adult believers are religiously motivated by what may be described as *insight.* That is, in a decision-making situation, Adult believers usually gather and evaluate pertinent information including what authorities say (Parent input) and how they feel about the situation (Child input); then they usually formulate their own thoughts, make a decision, and act upon it.

Adult believers are usually able to include a broader concern for others in their decisions because they are not compelled by duty or driven by impulse.

Adult believers give themselves away in conversation because they tend to discuss experiences as *unique* and *relative to a particular situation.* Unlike Parent believers who insist upon the absoluteness of the rule, Adult believers are more concerned with "thinking about the rule," "seeing if the rule is still helpful," "using the rule to clarify my own thoughts." Unlike Child believers, whose conversation is

filled with feeling words—joy, sorrow, happiness, guilt, freedom—
Adult believers will show much more interest in obtaining information, sharing experiences, asking questions, clarifying statements,
hearing other opinions, exploring alternate ways of behaving, getting things done.

A summary comparison of P-A-C believers and church activity is
given in figure 3.

FIGURE 3

P-A-C BELIEVERS AND CHURCH ACTIVITY

BELIEVERS	General mode of acting	Source of moral and ethical responsibility	Primary religious motivation	Characteristic way of talking about religion
PARENT BELIEVERS	*Judgmental* (obeying and enforcing rules) *and nurturing* (caring for needs)	*Traditional control,* simply carries out commands	*Duty,* obedience to the church	Tends to *absolutize,* "always," "never," "must," "should"
CHILD BELIEVERS	*Repressed, learned, impulsive,* or *intuitive* emotional response	*Response to feelings and conditioning,* does whatever natural or adapted feelings dictate	*Impulse, curiosity, approval* or *disapproval*	Tends to use words *laden with emotion*
ADULT BELIEVERS	*Reasonable,* clearly evaluating alternatives	*Internal control,* accepts full responsibility for behavior	*Insight,* reflectively formulates personal decisions	*Discusses experiences* as unique and relative to many different factors

Take a Moment

Make a list of five church activities that go on in your church.

**Would your parents participate in each activity? How does the
Child in you feel toward each activity? Independent of your**

feelings, what data do you have about the pros and cons of each activity?

Which of your ego states seem most involved in each activity? Does your involvement reflect anything about your religious beliefs?

4

HOW CAN A MAN BE BORN
WHEN HE IS OLD?

John 3:4

OK and NOT-OK Believers

FOUR LIFE-AS-A-WHOLE POSITIONS

How many people wish they could be born again?

How many times have people been heard saying, "I wish I could start my career all over" or "I'd like to have a second chance at raising a family" or "If I could only be sixteen again" or "I'd really be a better friend if I had another chance to try" or "I wish I had known when I was young what I know today."

Such people seem not to be lamenting some particular problem they may have or some particular mistake they may have made. Rather what they would like changed is their general approach to life. They wish to replace the poor, self-effacing view of themselves they now hold with a more positive, hopeful one.

How many people would like to be able to affirm what a discouraged teenager once cried out trying to preserve his own self-respect, "God made me, and he don't make junk!"

People want to feel good about themselves and others. The ways they do feel, according to Transactional Analysis theory, may be described in certain personal stances toward life-as-a-whole.

These general stances, usually adopted very early in life, involve self-acceptance or self-rejection and the acceptance or rejection of others. Or, in TA language, people describe themselves in general as OK or NOT-OK, and they evaluate others as OK or NOT-OK. Using these concepts, four general stances on life emerge, which are broad enough to include everyone from sociopaths to philanthropists.

THE FIRST LIFE-AS-A-WHOLE POSITION: *I'M OK—YOU'RE OK*

People in this life position are *mentally healthy*. Because they enjoy self-acceptance *(I'm OK)*, they feel free to express themselves, to set realistic goals and reach them. Such people are born to win and born to love. Because they accept others *(You're OK)*, they tend to get along well with people, to make many friends and few enemies. Tolerant and flexible, they generally do not demand perfection in others. This is the "get along with others" position; people in it feel "life is worthwhile."

THE SECOND LIFE-AS-A-WHOLE POSITION: *I'M OK—YOU'RE NOT-OK*

This describes people who are generally *arrogant* or *paranoid*. Because they often forcibly assert their self-acceptance *(I'm OK)*, they erroneously believe they are right while others are wrong; and they blame others, or at least criticize them, if things go badly. Because they are convinced that the rest of humanity is unacceptable *(You're NOT-OK)*, they usually drive away friends, spouses, children, and colleagues, or may seek others as targets for their persecution (physical and psychological) or for their constant critical advice. This is the "get rid of others" position; people in it express the feeling to others, "Your life is not worth much."

Almost everyone slips into this I'm OK—You're NOT-OK position now and again; for example, when people exonerate themselves and blame someone else, or when they strike back impulsively in a sense of self-justified anger, or when they play the Punishing Parent. But for most, this position is not a permanent attitude. Be careful, then, not to fasten such a label on anyone except those who clearly adopt I'm OK—You're NOT-OK consistently as a disposition toward almost everyone.

THE THIRD LIFE-AS-A-WHOLE POSITION: *I'M NOT-OK—YOU'RE OK*

This describes *depressive* or *discouraged* people, who think they are unlovable *(I'm NOT-OK)* and that only others are worthy of love *(You're OK)*. Because they cannot accept themselves, they frequently desert or withdraw or run away from others emotionally or physically; and they often refuse to take adequate responsibility for their own feelings and behavior. Because everyone else seems OK, depressive people may expect others to rescue them, to give them rewards and approval. This is the "get away from others" position. People in it feel "my life is not worth much."

Although babies may come into the world feeling OK, a series of NOT-OK experiences may influence many infants very early in life to adopt the position I'm NOT-OK—You're OK and to spend their entire lives in it. "How can I not be bad if big people say I am and punish me?" Because of an unhealthy perspective, they continue to collect only negative data about themselves: "I did it wrong again." "I'll never learn." "I never get the breaks." "I don't deserve the great boss I have." "My friends just tolerate me." Charlie Brown of *Peanuts* is a prime example of I'm NOT-OK—You're OK. It's no surprise that many people identify with this clumsy and inadequate creature who never seems to do anything right.

THE FOURTH LIFE-AS-A-WHOLE POSITION: *I'M NOT-OK—YOU'RE NOT-OK*

This describes people who find life an experience in *futility,* who are convinced that neither they nor anyone else is lovable. Because of their self-rejection *(I'm NOT-OK),* they feel incapable of doing anything right and conclude, "Why bother?" Because of their rejection of others *(You're NOT-OK)*, they feel as though no one and nothing else has anything good to offer either and conclude "nobody cares." "You can't trust anyone." This is the "get nowhere with others" position. People in it feel "life isn't worth anything at all."

In certain cases of I'm NOT-OK—You're NOT-OK, where psychological malnutrition has atrophied OK-feeling systems beyond repair, children may become autistic, sealing off all contact with the outside world, and adults may become schizophrenic or schizoid and, in extreme cases, commit suicide or homicide.

THINKING ABOUT THE FOUR LIFE-AS-A-WHOLE POSITIONS

On the basis of childhood experiences, people at a very early age take a stance toward life-as-a-whole and maintain this stance, usually at a feeling level, throughout life.

Life positions adopted by people influence their Parent, Adult, and Child ego states and underlie and color all interpersonal transactions.

Once a life position is adopted, experience is generally selectively interpreted to support it. Thus, I'm NOT-OK—You're OK persons receiving compliments may distort them in order to confirm their own NOT-OK position, saying, "She's just saying that to make me feel good, but both of us know that I'm NOT-OK and don't deserve the compliment!"

Life positions may be changed.

People were meant to live in the first life position: I'm OK—You're OK. Opting for this position involves a deliberate choice.

There is an important distinction between "choosing to be OK" and "feeling OK." The first describes a life position; the second describes the emotional quality of an experience. People in the first life position (I'm OK—You're OK) usually also *feel* OK, but sometimes they don't. Feeling NOT-OK in a particular situation does not cancel an OK life position, just as feeling OK in a situation does not cancel a NOT-OK life position.

Note that people in the first life position say "I'm OK" unconditionally. Others may say, "I'm OK *if* you . . ." or "I'm OK *when* you . . . ," but their assertion is the same as saying "I'm *NOT-OK unless* you . . ." which is a clear expression of the third life position, I'm NOT-OK—You're OK.

The decision to adopt an OK life position may be made at any time during one's life. It is never too late to do so. The Power Within is always available. The very desire to be OK is a sign of its continuous presence.

Those who have already made a decision to be OK, tentatively or definitively, may strengthen it by periodically reaffirming it. Reaffirmation seems to help keep the Inner Core open and its energies flowing.

Some people make the OK-decision in a single act. Others, less dramatically, seem slowly and imperceptibly to grow into OKness. Still others who have grown up in an OK atmosphere recognize the OK concept immediately, when it is presented, and affirm, "Of course, I'm OK."

Adopting the I'm OK—You're OK position involves, in some sense, a personal choice. No one can bestow OKness on another. Neither is being OK something that just happens by chance; it involves a decision: how I choose to view my life and how I choose to respond to others. Seeing myself as OK can be a conversion experience.

Take a Moment

As though watching yourself on a television screen, look at your life history. In general, in which of the four life-as-a-whole positions would you see yourself with regard to religious experience? Do you see yourself being OK, at ease, confident, healthy; or NOT-OK, fearful, anxious, depressed, discouraged? As you watch your personal religious history unfold, do you notice any radical change in your life position? Would you like to modify your life position in any way?

Transactional Analysis shows how people can change. It suggests ways that people can move from a NOT-OK life position toward an affirmation of OKness.

A genuine life-position change from NOT-OK to OK usually happens slowly, with much Adult encouragement and with much stroking—from self and others.

A stroke, says Berne, is "any act implying recognition of another's presence." Saying hello gives a stroke; returning a hello is a second stroke. Two strokes make a transaction.

If two or more people encounter each other, sooner or later one of them will speak or give some sign showing that they are aware of another's presence. This sign—usually a word or gesture—is called a *transactional stimulus.* The other's reaction is called a *transactional response.*

According to TA theory, the stimulus will be an expression of the person's Parent, Adult, or Child. The other person's response likewise expresses either his Parent, Adult, or Child.

When two Parents transact—labeled a P-P transaction—they may complain about everything from the weather to last Sunday's worship service and sermon. Or they talk nostalgically about the good old days when mugs of birch beer cost a nickel, and the church was strong, the clergy and the hymns more stirring. Or they may evaluate everyone from the bishop to the custodian. Helpful and supportive comments are likely to arise from a Nurturing Parent ego state, criticism and prejudicial statements from a Punishing Parent.

Child-Child transactions are often filled with emotional expressions. They include expressions of hate or love; things seem to be a breeze or a bother, superlatively easy or difficult. Child-Child conversations often run the entire gamut of feelings from exuberant joy to despairing depression. The exuberant joy is likely to be an expression of the Natural Child feeling OK; the despairing depression is likely to express the Adapted Child feeling NOT-OK.

Adult-Adult transactions are characterized by exchanges of information or know-how. Conversations among Adults focus on questions and answers. An A-A exchange is uncritical and uncomplaining and not laden with emotional overtones. Statements are usually centered responsibly in the here and now.

These are only a very few of the possible transactions that can happen between people.

Everybody hungers to be touched and to be recognized by others. Such hunger can be appeased with *strokes.*

Positive strokes may take the form of compliments, rewards, and approvals that generate satisfying feelings. They may involve actual physical touch or some symbolic contact such as a gesture, a glance, a written note, and so on—whatever says, "I know you're there, and you're OK." Positive strokes that produce OK feelings may range from a passerby's hello to expressions of deepest intimacy.

Negative strokes are whatever say, "I know you're there, and you're NOT-OK." They may take the form of reprimands, criticism, disapproval. Physically, negative strokes may include slapping, spanking, scowls, wagging fingers, and so on. Negative stroking usually produces NOT-OK feelings.

Often people's need to be touched and recognized goes unappeased because they receive neither positive nor negative strokes from others. This lack can detrimentally affect their personalities. People usually find *unrecognition* (no response from others) worse than receiving NOT-OK strokes (negative response), for the latter at least verify that they are here and alive, even if unwelcome.

It takes positive strokes to develop emotionally healthy people with a sense of OKness. Positive stroke-giving is a skill that can be learned and practiced. Stroking experts are necessary in homes, offices, schools, churches—wherever people want to become OK or to stay OK.

Take a Moment

What was one of the nicest things ever said or done to you when you were little? If you can't remember anything nice, what did you wish had been said or done to you? The positive strokes you received or longed for when you were little are the ones you most probably look for now.

What was one of the worst things ever said or done to you when you were little? If you can't remember anything like this, what did you sense might be the worst thing that could have been said or done to you? The negative strokes you received or feared are the ones you more probably try to avoid now.

OKNESS AND BELIEVERS

Corresponding to the four life positions, there are four religious stances which believers can adopt, four general ways that believers tend to look at life and religion. These four stances, broad enough to include everyone from belligerent atheists to mellowed saints, parallel the four life positions and take their names from them:

The First Religious Stance: I'm OK—You're OK
(The Confident Believer)

The Second Religious Stance: I'm OK—You're NOT-OK
(The Superiority Believer)

The Third Religious Stance: I'm NOT-OK—You're OK
(The Anxious Believer)

The Fourth Religious Stance: I'm NOT-OK—You're NOT-OK
(The Despairing Believer)

THE CONFIDENT BELIEVER *(I'M OK—YOU'RE OK)*

I'm OK—You're OK believers display a *hopeful* and *confident* attitude toward life. They find life worth living, filled with meaning and purpose. Their Inner Core is open and free. Learning to detect signs of growth and progress in the world, they discover unsuspected capacities for love and trust in themselves and others. They are in touch with the Power Within. Confident Believers can find religious satisfaction in watching a sunset, holding a baby, working in the garden, or playing a hand of pinochle with long-time friends.

In their attitude toward others, I'm OK—You're OK believers recognize that people can be great, caring, interesting. They like to see everyone as uniquely important and essential to God's work in the world. Like good shepherds, they value searching for the one lost sheep. Since they view everyone as OK, every transaction for them is a possible growth experience.

Characteristic feelings of Confident Believers include being positive, accepting, and open to the world. Sensitive to changes happening within themselves and all around them, they are curious and inquisitive. Their viewpoint is generally positive, having no need to be hateful or punishing or anxious, for they believe that deep down things are OK. Even though people slip back into feeling NOT-OK from time to time, or have a tenuous hold on their OKness, the Confident Believer usually trusts that OK feelings will ultimately transform anyone who allows these feelings to grow inside. OK believers can be accepting of others, however they may think and act, because they affirm that God's love and forgiveness operates uniquely for every individual. John the Evangelist, Confident Believer in touch with the Power Within, wrote of God, "His light shines in the darkness and the shadow cannot overcome that light."

Since OK believers feel OK in their relation to God, they find it easy to accept every other person as a special expression of God's love at work. Jesus allowed Zaccheus to feel OK by touching his Inner

Core. In turn, Zaccheus was able to accept others as valuable and important, and, as an expression of this, he repaid fourfold the money he had illegally taken from others.[1] He was born again.

Confident Believers affirm that God says you're OK to everyone. They believe they are loved by God, and they often act on that conviction. They have light and don't always hide it under a bushel basket. They have talents and don't always bury them; they have loaves and fishes and are usually willing to share.

The Confident Believer's religious stance is based on *faith, reflection,* and *action.*

The decision to accept God's word, You're OK, often requires *faith,* especially when, for one reason or another, NOT-OK feelings are strongly experienced. Such feelings may involve replays of old NOT-OK recordings from the Punishing Parent or Adapted Child, or they may be the result of others radiating NOT-OK feelings. OKness is precious, but fragile, and needs to be guarded and strengthened. Sometimes new OK persons find it difficult to maintain OKness; for example, they may receive Parent criticism for backsliding. Such OK persons, like small children learning how to walk, need encouragement from others.

Entering the I'm OK—You're OK believer's stance invites *reflection* and evaluation. Once the new stance is chosen, I'm OK—You're OK believers are free to begin reviewing past Parent and Child recordings, to turn off those that support NOT-OK stances, and to update those that could help reinforce the new stance.

The confident religious stance is also characterized by decision and *action.* OK believers realize there is much to be done. The list is long and challenging: personal growth, enrichment of others, new levels of relating to other people and to God, transforming the earth, and all the changes needed to help heal, build, and shape human communities and the physical environment.

OK believers believe they have the best reasons in life for living. They feel free to be themselves. Confident Believers often develop innovative ways to live, ways to experience deeply the Power Within. Even when they have questions or doubts about beliefs, they look at them with their confident Adult in charge of the exploration.

THE SUPERIORITY BELIEVER *(I'M OK—YOU'RE NOT-OK)*

This second religious stance tends to generate believers who manifest an attitude of *superiority* over others, which, in extreme cases, reaches hatred of anything beside themselves or their religious clique. In children, this stance is encouraged in games like "Mine is better" or "That's not for you to know" or "Too bad you're not on top, like me." Punishing Parent believers can very easily find themselves adopting this better-than-thou religious posture. The overnurturing Parent can also express an I'm OK—You're NOT-OK attitude in expressions such as "Here, let me do it for you, dear" (Read: "You're incompetent") or "How could we expect someone like you to be able to do that, poor thing?"

Believers who say, "I'm OK—You're NOT-OK," may, like Pharisees, develop attitudes of disdain and scorn toward others "who do not know the law and the Scriptures as we do." Such believers may publicly flaunt their theological acumen or moral observance. They may communicate the You're NOT-OK message to others by avoiding them, not sitting near them in church, looking disparagingly at their way of dress, criticizing their worldly language, accusing them of being inadequate members of the church. Unlike Confident Believers who tend to give positive strokes, the Superiority Believer is master at giving negative strokes. These I'm OK—You're NOT-OK believers lack sensitivity toward others.

In extreme cases, Superiority Believers tend to be destructive. Tyrannical personalities may brutalize their own children, spouses, friends, and fellow church members, thus helping to spawn another generation of religious people who hate. Certain extreme Superiority Believers might enjoy wielding clubs, guns, and torches as members of a religious police force, threatening the lives of believers who differ from them.

Such Superiority Believers may absolve themselves of any moral obligations. From an outsider's point of view, these people lack a conscience; from their point of view, however, *whatever they do* is morally right. Some Superiority Believers will exempt themselves from all moral law saying, "That doesn't apply to me," or else may appoint themselves as models of the perfect conscience.

Characteristically, I'm OK—You're NOT-OK believers often feel *superior* and *self-justifying*. They may feel superior because they are the only OK believers in the world and so the only ones who deserve to be alive and walk on the earth. They usually have no trouble justifying themselves in everything they do, for they are a law unto themselves: Truth means *their truth*. Frequently they create their own moral laws and theological doctrines. Consequently, such believers seldom experience religious doubts or discuss theological questions. Whoever refuses to comply with their interpretations of the Bible may be punished and reprimanded.

Beneath what appears to be a holy countenance, Superiority Believers are often hard and tough. Since they see others attempting to make them feel NOT-OK, they tenaciously hold on to their self-induced OKness. In such cases, though an ingratiating smile appears on the surface, inside the message is more likely to be "That little runt of a sinner! How dare he accuse me! I'll teach him a lesson he'll never forget!"

Certain religious groups collectively adopt the superiority stance, "We're OK—everyone else is NOT-OK." More familiar comparisons of us to them might be: "We're right, they're wrong" or "Ours is the best church" or "You can't be saved unless you belong to our church." Extreme forms of the superiority religious stance occur in groups such as the Ku Klux Klan, Witch Hunters, Inquisitors, Crusaders, and the like.

If Superiority Believers were asked about salvation or their relation to God, some might put God on their side and think something like, "It's people like me who'll be sitting among the chosen ones." *(God and I are OK—everyone else is NOT-OK.)*

Other Superiority Believers might push the question of salvation aside with a wave of the hand, "I'm not concerned whether or not God says I'm OK. I don't need salvation, I'm perfectly satisfied with the way I am, and don't need any God to declare me OK." *("I'm OK—God and all the rest of the world are NOT-OK.")*

In the first case, the believer has God on his side against everyone else. In the second, the believer includes God with the rest of the NOT-OK world.

THE ANXIOUS BELIEVER *(I'M NOT-OK—YOU'RE OK)*

Anxious Believers most often assume attitudes of *insecurity* and *inferiority* toward life in general—"I'm helpless and inadequate, my life isn't worth much"—and these feelings frequently carry over into religious life. For example, Anxious Believers may feel uncertain that they're doing things correctly. One may call up the pastor to see if it's all right to write a letter to his congressman encouraging prison reform. Others may refuse responsibilities in the church or at work because they're afraid they will fail; and even if they accept the responsibility and do a fine job, Anxious Believers will tend to focus on their inadequacies, perhaps announcing a list of things that went wrong, adding, "Mr. Smith would have done the job so much better than I."

The Anxious Believer's attitude toward others, since they're all OK, is that they must be better off than he is. "Jim has all that training in theology; Mary has missionary experience in Africa; Fred has been a member of the vestry for years; John knows how to build an effective committee; Phyllis got her picture in the newspaper after her work on the inner-city housing project. And in all these years, I've done nothing. Everyone's a better and stronger believer than I."

Looking up to others, often unrealistically, an Anxious Believer may favor the religious opinions of others and substitute their evaluations for his own. I'm NOT-OK—You're OK believers seek approval from others, as if a good word from an OK person would relieve their anxiety and make them better religious people. But usually strokes from OK believers generate only momentary OK feelings. As soon as the stroking effects wear off, anxiety returns, and the NOT-OK believers may be more convinced than ever of their own insecurity and inferiority.

Characteristically, NOT-OK believers feel inadequate and discouraged. While others seem to find personal satisfaction and support in their religion, Anxious Believers seem to reap only weeds —failures, sins, doubts, temptations, feeling stupid about religion and inadequate in religious experience. Some Anxious Believers may find going to church a bore; others experience only distractions when they try to pray; others find reading the Bible a threatening experience. Meanwhile, they see others finding love, joy, and hope in religious experience. The contrast makes the Anxious Believer even more anxious and upset than before.

As one NOT-OK believer put it, "At church I look around. People seem rapt in prayer, enthusiastically singing, in touch with God. For years, I have wished for experiences like these, something that would satisfy my deepest self. But instead I recognize the same old emptiness inside. And I feel deeply discouraged."

In general, NOT-OK believers work out their religious lives in fear and trembling. Hell and punishment may loom large in their perspective. They wonder, "How can God ever say to me, 'You're OK'?" They speculate, "Maybe I'll never be saved."

During a sermon on God's love, some Anxious Believers find themselves concentrating on the few words about sin that the minister speaks. Other NOT-OK believers, reading books that describe human failings and sinfulness, may instantly apply these negative qualities to themselves. The search for satisfying religious experience is a difficult upward climb for many Anxious Believers, like a continual attempt to keep from sliding back into the hell of NOT-OKness. Some simply affirm, "I am not worthy," and refuse to allow the Power Within to flow through their Inner Core.

The third religious stance (I'm NOT worthy—Everyone else is) is a very common position among today's believers. It is perhaps most familiar among Christians who refuse to hear the words of God's unconditional loving acceptance as expressed in the parables of the prodigal son and the woman at the well. In the face of God's loving invitations, some Anxious Believers may reply, "God can't mean me" or "Other people maybe, but I don't deserve it" or I'm not a saint yet." They may chastise themselves with prayers such as "I am not worthy enough to pick up the crumbs under your table" or "Depart from me for I am a sinful man, O Lord."

People in this position tend to hear selectively and read what supports their NOT-OK religious stance. Doubters will find more evidence to remain doubtful; those discouraged will find material to support their discouragement; the anxious will collect facts and theories to heighten their anxiety.

Since so many religious people adopt an I'm NOT-OK—You're OK stance, there is no dearth of words or writing to nourish this unhealthy position and keep it thriving in religious groups.

THE DESPAIRING BELIEVER *(I'M NOT-OK—YOU'RE NOT-OK)*

The attitude toward life of believers who adopt this fourth general religious stance is one of *hopelessness*. Denying the Power Within, they believe there is no OKness within themselves; and because they view everyone else also without OKness, perhaps even God, there is no one to bestow OKness on them or on anyone else. "Life is worthless," they say, "and we can't do anything about it." Feeling overwhelmed, they tend to despair in every way.

Frequently, such Despairing Believers suffer from a history of extreme stroking deprivation. They may have received few if any positive religious strokes as infants and children and, like a plant whose roots have already withered, seem incapable now of absorbing any nourishment.

Since they see how ineffective positive strokes are to them, Despairing Believers may conclude that it is worthless for them to stroke others.

As a rule their relationships are devoid of joy and happiness. Accordingly, their attitude toward others is, "Nobody's OK. Nobody can do anything to fix things up."

Those who adopt this despairing position more strongly may feel, "Everyone is out to hurt and destroy whomever they can. No one, including God, is really concerned about anyone else."

A pessimistic believer but faithful churchgoer announced, "Look at all the miracles Jesus performed. And the people treated him no better than the feature attraction at a sideshow. The crowds didn't want to be affected or converted; they wanted only to be entertained."

"Things on earth aren't any better than they were in the time of Noah," an old woman told her pastor, "when God decided the best thing he could do was destroy the earth."

Despairing, Nobody's-OK Believers tend to nurture feelings of defeat and frequently show coldness toward others. Their actions often betray an I-give-up attitude or one that says, "Keep your distance."

Many Despairing Believers are cold-feeling because they are convinced that people have no warmth. Any displays of love and affection toward them may be interpreted as hypocrisy. Or as one woman put it, "When it seems like somebody is really caring for you, just look behind their actions and you'll see there's a selfish motive at work."

Many Despairing Believers, convinced that contact with others merely increases the grand total of NOT-OK feelings in the world, prefer to hide, to keep everyone at a distance. Some might say, "Every time I go out into the world of people, I return to my room less human."

Other Despairing Believers are overtly punishing. According to them, since nobody's OK, everyone deserves to be taken to task for their evil and wickedness. As a result, they view everyone as punishers—mothers, fathers, sisters, brothers, friends, clergymen, even Jesus—and they join in the destructive games. "Kill or be killed is the rule," they may say. "If you're going to make me feel NOT-OK, I'm going to punish you right back."

In both cases, as cowards or commandos, these fourth-stance believers are despairing because they believe the human race is plummeting downward in a tailspin toward destruction. They are convinced life can't get any better, that it can only get worse.

When asked about their attitudes toward salvation and their relation to God, Despairing Believers are likely to reply, "I can't be saved. Nobody will be saved. We're all rotten to the core. What God says to all of us is 'You're NOT-OK.' "

"When I think of religion at all," wrote Oscar Wilde in a time of disbelief, "I feel as if I would like to found an order for those who cannot believe; the Confraternity of all the Fatherless one might call it, where on an altar on which no taper burned, a priest, in whose heart peace had no dwelling might celebrate with unblessed bread and a chalice empty of wine."

Before Wilde died, he reestablished touch with the Power Within and experienced the peace and joy of a Confident Believer. He was born again.

Figure 4 summarizes the four general religious stances and their corresponding characteristic attitudes.

Take a Moment

Imagine four persons each in a different life-as-a-whole position, a Confident Believer, a Superiority Believer, an Anxious Believer, and a Despairing Believer. Then write a short prayer as each believer might say it. Compare the four prayers.

FIGURE 4

LIFE-AS-A-WHOLE RELIGIOUS STANCES
AND
THEIR CORRESPONDING ATITUDES

BELIEVER'S GENERAL RELIGIOUS STANCE	Attitude toward life in general	Attitude toward other people	Characteristic religious feelings	Attitude toward salvation
CONFIDENT BELIEVERS I'm OK—God and others are OK.	Life *is* worth living.	People are great—caring, interesting, fun.	I feel open to the whole world.	I know that all creation is saved, including you and me.
SUPERIORITY BELIEVERS I'm OK— others are not OK (God may be OK or NOT-OK).	I'm important, but your life isn't worth much.	Too bad other people don't understand the way things are.	People don't know enough to take my advice.	I'm the only one who deserves to be saved (God OK) or I don't need salvation (God NOT-OK).
ANXIOUS BELIEVERS I'm NOT-OK —God and others are OK.	I'm helpless and inferior; my life isn't worth much.	You're strong and superior, better off than I am.	I feel anxious, inadequate, stupid.	I have to work out my life in fear and trembling.
DESPAIRING BELIEVERS I'm NOT-OK —God and others are NOT-OK.	Life isn't worth much, and I couldn't possibly do anything about it.	Nobody can do anything to fix things up.	I give up. Keep your distance.	I can't be saved.

5

WHO THEN IS A FAITHFUL SERVANT OF THE LORD?

See Matt. 24:45

The Ways and Whys of Believers

WHAT CAN I DO?

People spend much of their lives doing things to please others. They may say, "What's next on your list?" "Is there anything you need?" "Can I give you a ride?" "What would you like me to do?"

What people do often reveals who they are and what motivates them. Their deeds help shape their personalities and also their religious lives.

"What does God want me to do?"

Believers want to be faithful, sensible, and wise servants of the Lord and often wonder "What can I do to please him?"

Psychologically, believers' activities and motives are strongly influenced by the life-as-a-whole stance they take. Being OK or NOT-OK explains much about the ways and whys of believers.

The first religious stance seems to be the only one in which believers make ethical choices that are *fully conscious* and *based on reflection,* that is, experience, information, and feelings are evaluated and brought to decision.

Confident Believers are usually willing to accept responsibility for their behavior and feelings. Despite a possible sea of NOT-OK feelings in and around them, they consciously choose to believe that in their Inner Core they are OK. "Although we may have many faults and weaknesses, we're OK people nonetheless." Convinced that God loves and accepts them as they are, they can afford to be positive, open, accepting. Their openness is further supported by knowing that "there are people in the world who genuinely value me as important." Being OK is the fundamental perspective from which they choose to live. Confident Believers think about what being a faithful servant is and act on it.

Confident Believers are willing to experiment and explore. Their ethical codes are not merely negative—to avoid sin and to carry out duties—but tend to be much more focused on positive creative things they are capable of doing. They are ready to find new ways to show their love, their social awareness, their own desire to grow spiritually and develop.

OK believers feel free to explore new forms of prayer and worship in hopes of finding new ways to help others in their own religious lives. "God gave us the world," they might say, "to deal lovingly and creatively with everything on it. What a wonderful challenge!"

In behavior and in conversation, OK believers usually strike others as people who *establish reasonable goals.* Characteristically, they are also interested in the present and the future of the community, willingly cooperate in church projects, keep their enthusiasm and interest high for social action, and show a willingness to adapt when situations require it.

Confident Believers are good to have as group members in church activities. In discussions they frequently ask helpful questions and usually possess useful information that they are willing to share. People enjoy working with OK believers. "By this all men will know that you are my disciples, if you have love for one another."[1]

Religiously, Confident Believers seldom waste energy nourishing useless guilt feelings. They are usually genuinely sorry when they do something wrong or offend someone, and can accept forgiveness and with renewed vigor direct their energies to the shared tasks at hand. They tend to see others as capable and good even though others may find it difficult to view themselves as positively as the OK believers do.

THE WHYS OF CONFIDENT BELIEVERS *(I'M OK—YOU'RE OK)*

I'm OK—You're OK believers enjoy almost unlimited sources of positive motivation. They firmly believe that *people can change and grow* and that everyone is capable of higher and higher levels of self-actualization. For this reason, many Confident Believers study psychology and the ways of human development; others may enter social work, teaching, counseling, the ministry; still others may get involved in shared interests and hobbies. OK believers are usually able to see all these interests, and many more, as ways to help people change and grow.

I'm OK—You're OK believers seem to find hope in every situation. Convinced that being OK is the greatest asset to life, they would like as many people as possible to share the I'm OK—You're OK religious stance with them.

One of the Confident Believers' strongest positive motivations is *helping people stay OK.* They know that people's convictions and beliefs, including their own, can be very fragile. With all the NOT-OK-feeling people around, contamination is bound to occur. As a consequence, OK believers are usually interested in learning ways to nourish OKness in themselves and others. They may search for opportunities to give positive strokes to others to help the Power Within come fully alive in everyone.

"I made known to them thy name," Jesus prayed to the Father, "and I will make it known, that the love with which thou has loved me may be in them, and I in them."[2]

On the other hand, realizing that there is *never any need to make others feel NOT-OK,* OK believers are motivated to avoid giving negative strokes or doing things that might communicate NOT-OK judgments upon other people.

Confident believers tend to avoid engaging in the destructive games that people often play. Usually, when someone initiates a game that is bound to end up making people feel NOT-OK, Confident Believers try to turn the game into an honest and productive transaction.

After reprimanding the Pharisees, Jesus counseled his disciples not to imitate their superiority games. Jesus wished there to be no pecking order among the apostles. "He who is greatest among you shall be your servant."[3]

THE WAYS OF SUPERIORITY BELIEVERS *(I'M OK—YOU'RE NOT-OK)*

I'm OK—You're NOT-OK believers tend to develop a moral system of which they are the center and in which they view their wishes as absolute commandments. Superiority Believers think they and others like them are *the* only faithful servants. Such superiority attitudes usually arise in people in one of two ways.

First, certain people may become Superiority Believers because of the continual hateful treatment they received during childhood at the hands of brutalizing parents and other grown-ups. The only time such children feel OK is when they are left alone—"I'm OK as long as I'm alone," says the beaten child. "Everyone else is NOT-OK and is trying to make me NOT-OK like them, but I'll show them; I'll be OK *by myself.*"

Second, certain people may become Superiority Believers because they received continually favorable comparison during childhood, for example, "You're smarter, better, nicer, holier . . . than everyone else." This kind of conditioning may lead a person to adopt the position, "I'm better and more valuable than anyone else in the world."

The quality of moral choice in Superiority Believers is *unreflective* because it generally springs from a conditioning process begun in childhood. They had to adopt superior behavior because it was forced upon them by others, either through beatings or continually favorable comparison.

Such believers have never allowed themselves honestly to look at the way things are. Without trial, they may have condemned the world and everyone in it, except themselves.

For some, this verdict was probably delivered back at age three when they lay in a crib after a beating; and the world has never been brought to trial again.

For others, the verdict may also have been delivered back at age three when an overzealous mommy assured her youngster, "Always remember that nobody else in the world is as good and nice as my perfect baby. You're lovely, and the rest of the world is horrid." The youngster probably immediately agreed, unreflectively, and the condemnation of the world has been sustained without question since that moment and throughout life.

Since Superiority Believers characteristically make unreflective moral decisions (without consulting their Adult), they can hardly be said to be enjoying freedom of conscience (an almost exclusively Adult activity).

In behavior and conversation, Superiority Believers communicate their I'm OK—You're NOT-OK message in many ways. Generally, they feel *no compunction at destroying the lives and hopes of others.* At times, like huge ugly giants, they may stomp about the world, verbally slashing with bloody swords anyone within reach. Frequently their words shower blame and condemnation upon others and approval upon themselves and their ways.

No one, it seems, can do anything worthy of their approval. Even when they may reluctantly pay a compliment, others learn to watch for the barb attached to the end of it. "You did the job all right this time, Charlie, but if I know you, you'll make a mess of it next time."

Often no one or nothing ranks as more important than their wishes and feelings. Superiority clergy or church officials may even cultivate or hire a string of people to smile and approve everything they do. Any underling who dares to contradict them might just as well take the next bus home and never come back to that church again.

Jesus observed the Pharisees using we're-superior tactics upon the Jewish people of his day. "They preach," he said, "but do not practice. [*Superiority Believers exempt themselves from moral obligation.*] They bind heavy burdens, hard to bear, and lay them on other people's shoulders [*Superiority Believers view their wishes as absolute commands*]; but they themselves will not move them with their finger." [*Superiority Believers see themselves at the center and head of their moral system.*]4

THE WHYS OF SUPERIORITY BELIEVERS: *(I'M OK—YOU'RE NOT-OK)*

I'm OK—You're NOT-OK believers tend to appear superior and tough and often act as though they are the only OK persons in the world. "I've got the answer," they might say. "I know because I made the rules and I interpret them." Often they are motivated to continue being superior because they are convinced that the church would fall apart without them.

Many Superiority Believers, even though they wear religious garb, care not one whit about God because, by no stretch of their imagination, can even God be more important than they are. "I'm OK, God," they might say. "I can judge myself. And you, God, are NOT-OK because you really don't know what the score is."

Of course from time to time other people challenge their superior position. Religious people often discover that other religious people also think themselves to be supreme; and this may lead to a test of strength. Religious history leaves a trail of believers executed by Inquisitions, Witch Hunters, Crusaders, and the like. In ordinary situations Superiority Believers might say, "Others may try to change me, but I'm hard and tough. I'll show them who's right."

I'm OK—You're NOT-OK believers have strong negative motivation, too. Remember, some Superiority Believers may have been beaten all through infancy and childhood, while others may have been continually favored over other children. Despite protestations of supreme power, as grown-ups the beaten ones still experience beatings and the favored ones still experience disappointments of various sorts. For example, if the clever move they may have planned didn't come off as expected, they may argue that the weather seems against them or age and sickness is driving them to fury. Some Superiority Believers prefer to deny a high fever rather than admit they're finite and human. "I can lick my own wounds," one says, reminiscent of a brutal infancy. "I can comfort myself; I'll be all right if you just leave me alone."

THE WAYS OF ANXIOUS BELIEVERS *(I'M NOT-OK—YOU'RE OK)*

Anxious Believers often make moral choices strongly influenced by their negative self-image. Following thousands of negative impressions recorded in the brain since infancy—"Can't you ever do anything right?" or "Your brother is better than you" or "I can't trust you"—such people frequently make *unreflective ethical decisions.* Their choices are often based on overwhelming feeling-convictions of inadequacy, inferiority, and unworthiness: "I've always been wrong, so I must be wrong again" or "I've never done anything good" or "I'm not lovable."

Even though they believe God says humans are OK in general, Anxious Believers usually cannot persuade themselves that God's loving acceptance applies to them. Anxious Believers continually worry about whether or not they are faithful enough to the Lord.

Since Anxious Believers almost constantly feel NOT-OK—and don't like it—they remain on the lookout for ways to get OK feelings. They are, as a rule, convinced that OK feelings can only come from OK people; so they look around for whoever will give them as many strokes as possible.

Yet often their NOT-OK state is so deeply ingrained that all the stroking they get never makes them the OK people they so desperately want to be. A shower of positive strokes which might put an OK person into a permanent state of ecstasy seems to run off the Anxious Believer like water off a proverbial duck's back.

No matter how positive or frequent, stroking will never *make* NOT-OK people OK as they hope it will. People are not made OK simply by a series of good feelings or simply by someone else telling them they're OK. According to TA psychology, becoming OK involves a personal deliberate choice allowing the Power Within to flow through the Inner Core. Choosing OKness seems to be precisely what Anxious Believers never do; instead, they wait in vain for someone or something outside themselves to *make them OK.*

In behavior and conversation, I'm NOT-OK—You're OK believers, typically say or do *anything that will make them feel OK,* even momentarily. This often involves making others feel NOT-OK. "After all," certain Anxious Believers may argue, "it offers a bit of relief to know that someone else is in a NOT-OK state as well as I."

Some I'm NOT-OK believers may aggressively stand up for a personal opinion and sometimes even fight to defend it, but more often they withdraw from the argument, preferring to defer, or give in, or give up. "I'm usually wrong," one might say, "so I must be wrong again."

Anxious Believers may often be found lamenting their moral weakness, their inability to stick to resolutions, their failure to improve, their lack of good feelings. One complains, "I still confess the same old faults and sins that bothered me years ago. I'm no better than I was." They tend to view other believers as more religious than they, having deeper faith, able to carry on with life more cheerfully and more successfully.

Typical faults of Anxious Believers may include discouragement, impatience, jealousy, envy, fear, and loneliness. As a rule, the loneliness of Anxious Believers is not an existential aloneness, but a destructive game operating between Punishing Parent and NOT-OK Child.

The Loneliness Game seems to go like this: When an Anxious Believer does something worthy of notice, his Child may say to his Parent, "Didn't I do a nice job on the church program?" And the Parent within him answers, "It was pretty good, but it could have been much better." This reinforces his Child's NOT-OK feelings as well as his social unacceptability. "If I disapprove of myself," argues the Child, "how can anyone else think well of me?" Next time around, when the Anxious Believer runs the church program even better than before, his Child hoping for a stroke from his Parent asks, "Didn't I do a better job this time?" And the Parent within him replies as usual, "Yes, but it was not good enough." Once again the NOT-OK Child is left to sink deeper into NOT-OK quicksand. Anxiously, the Child immediately applies the condemnation to his entire life. "I'm *never* good enough," he says. "No wonder *nobody* likes me. No wonder I'm lonely." The Loneliness Game is purely an inner dialogue; it requires no other players.

THE WHYS OF ANXIOUS BELIEVERS *(I'M NOT-OK—YOU'RE OK)*

Positive motivation for Anxious Believers (I'm helpless—You're strong) tends to center around their *need to build up a self-estimate* and their related *need to be approved by others.* Recall that Anxious Believers usually feel insecure and inferior. Their fragile self-confidence can be short-circuited easily; and they become fearful, discouraged, and less than ever satisfied with themselves. Since they tend to see others as better than they are, they often look to others for approval, much as a baby looks to grown-ups for approval.

From sad experience they know that the effect of ninety-nine positive strokes may sometimes be wiped out by a single negative stroke.

Anxious Believers also utilize negative motivation. Soon in life they may discover that if they get there first or receive the biggest prize they somehow feel, momentarily at least, less NOT-OK than they did before. But even when they harass people from other churches, get higher grades on a Bible quiz, give more money to the poor, or build a bigger church, Anxious Believers *expect* eventually to feel NOT-OK about their behavior. And their expectations are usually fulfilled.

Some Anxious Believers discover that another quick way to avoid NOT-OK feelings is to laugh at the other guy's mistakes or gloat over his failures. Other Anxious Believers may sometimes put on a mask of confidence or competence to hide their NOT-OK feelings. Still others may become highly competitive, again usually to hide anxious feelings.

THE WAYS OF DESPAIRING BELIEVERS *(I'M NOT-OK—YOU'RE NOT OK)*

Despairing Believers also lead a *nonreflective moral life.* In their eyes all humanity seems doomed to failure and NOT-OKness; their ethical thinking is usually contaminated by a cold, despairing attitude. "There is no hope," they say, "so why keep looking." Despairing Believers either doubt that anyone could be faithful or doubt the existence of God, and conclude that there is nothing to be faithful about. Since they believe that no one will be approved and that no one on earth can fix things up, many Despairing Believers simply have as their goal "to get through life."

Since they often find life itself painful and religion an embarrassment, some Despairing Believers may be *fond of punishing and criticizing others,* hoping to silence them or at least keep them out of the way. "If they learn what a beast I am," he reasons, "maybe they'll stay away from me. I've got enough troubles of my own without piling other people's discouragement on my back."

Like any NOT-OK person, the Despairing Believer dislikes getting involved. While Anxious Believers may avoid getting involved because they feel people will reject them or they're afraid they will fail, Despairing Believers are more than likely convinced that human interaction will only bring a new storm of NOT-OK feelings upon everyone involved—which no one needs.

For this reason, Despairing Believers sometimes throw wrenches in projects that require their participation. "It will never work," one might say, "for the following fifteen reasons. And if you do get it to work, it will create fifteen unhelpful results. I vote against it." Another might say, "Why can't we just keep doing things the old way? Everybody's used to the old way. Then no one's life will be upset any more than it is already."

At other times, the despairer's NOT-OK Child withdraws and regresses. "I can't take any more abuse from that minister at his religious service. I think I'll go out and get drunk. Maybe I can forget about the whole thing." Other versions of withdrawal might be expressed in "I need a vacation from church" or "Don't bother me about God" or "I don't want to pray. Just let me sit here in peace and quiet."

THE WHYS OF DESPAIRING BELIEVERS *(I'M NOT-OK—YOU'RE NOT-OK)*

I'm NOT-OK—You're NOT-OK believers, locked into negativisms such as hopelessness and despair, have little positive motivation to allow the Power Within to flow. Viewing life as a dead-end street, their best statement may sound something like, *"IF I can just make it through life* with a minimum of negative feelings!" Sometimes, like the man with chronic migraine headaches, Despairing Believers survive from day to day; they get through life hour by hour. Yet, because their despair extends across the boundary of death, they may be convinced of their damnation, God's rejection of them, endless eons of punishment and suffering awaiting them— or that there's nothing after life. For them, hell will be no different from life on earth; they will have to get through it hour by hour.

Despairing Believers are strong and clear on negative motivation. They usually try to *avoid the punishment and destructiveness of others.* Often their password is *avoidance.* Many withdraw, becoming impenetrable as steel. When people try to get them involved, they do everything in their power to avoid it. Despairing Believers are sometimes like bumblebees, they won't sting unless you provoke them.

In seeming contrast, sometimes Despairing Believers plunge into social activity. But usually their motive is to disrupt it, for they believe that interaction breeds more and more NOT-OKness in everybody. "Since everybody's NOT-OK to begin with," they might argue, "people would be better off to sit quietly like rocks waiting for time to pass."

Figure 5 presents a comparison of the ways believers behave, and figure 6 summarizes the positive and negative motivations believers use in the four general religious stances.

Take a Moment [5]

A pastor was trying to figure out the biblical story of the Good Samaritan from the standpoint of Transactional Analysis. In his pocket was a preliminary outline for a sermon that read:

Traveler: I'm NOT-OK—You're OK (Anxious Believer)

Priest & Levite: I'm OK—You're NOT-OK (Superiority Believers)

Robbers: I'm NOT-OK—You're NOT-OK (Despairing Believers)

Good Samaritan: I'm OK—You're OK (Confident Believer)

Do you agree with the pastor's analysis? How does it tie in with the question raised in the title of this Chapter?

FIGURE 5

THE WAYS OF BELIEVERS

BELIEVER'S GENERAL RELIGIOUS STANCE	*Quality of moral choice*	*Typical kinds of religious behavior and conversation*
ONFIDENT ELIEVERS m OK—God nd others are ▸K.	Conscious and reflective: based on experience, information, etc.	Willing to change; willing to cooperate; establish reasonable goals; interested in the future; ask helpful questions; possess useful information, etc.
UPERIORITY ELIEVERS m OK—others e not OK (God ay be OK or ▸OT-OK).	Unreflective: based on continual superior or authoritarian behavior encouraged by others during childhood (and later)	Buy own "yes men." Feel no compunction at destroying others' lives. Always blaming others, justifying themselves, etc.
NXIOUS ELIEVERS m NOT-OK— ▸od and others ·e OK.	Unreflective: based on negative impressions of self received during childhood (and later)	Say and do whatever will make self feel more OK, for example, making others feel NOT-OK. Bemoaning same old faults and NOT-OKness, etc.
▸ESPAIRING ELIEVERS m NOT-OK— ·od and others ·e NOT-OK.	Unreflective: based on lack of positive response from others during childhood (and later)	Punish and criticize everyone; sometimes withdraw and regress; may throw wrenches into group activities, etc.

FIGURE 6

WHAT MOTIVATES BELIEVERS

BELIEVER'S GENERAL RELIGIOUS STANCE	*Positive Motivation* (religious and general)	*Negative Motivation* (religious and general)
CONFIDENT BELIEVERS I'm OK—God and others are OK.	People can change and grow; everyone is capable of self-actualization; we can help each other stay OK.	I can avoid playing destructive "games people play"; I have no need to make others feel NOT-OK.
SUPERIORITY BELIEVERS I'm OK—others are not OK (God may be OK or NOT-OK).	I'm the only one who's right and good. Others try to defeat me, but I'm hard and tough.	I can lick my own wounds. I can comfort myself. I'll be all right if you just leave me alone.
ANXIOUS BELIEVERS I'm NOT-OK—God and others are OK.	I need to build up my self estimate. I need to be approved by others.	I try to avoid feeling NOT-OK by laughing at other's mistakes. If I've got to feel NOT-OK, I'll make others feel that way too.
DESPAIRING BELIEVERS I'm NOT-OK—God and others are NOT-OK.	If I can just get through life—day by day, hour by hour.	If the world doesn't respond to me, I won't respond to it. I'm simply trying to avoid punishment and the destructiveness of others.

6

HOW SHALL WE SING THE LORD'S SONG IN A STRANGE LAND?

Ps. 137:4

Staying a Confident Believer

In translating the Book of Genesis, Martin Luther commented, "All of life is a crossing of the Red Sea." As he reflected on the story of the Hebrew exodus from Egyptian captivity, he saw how religious experience was a continual growth from slavery to freedom, or as Paul the apostle expressed it, "For freedom we were made free."[1]

In TA language, this means finding the Power Within—the Power at the Bottom of the Well—that will carry us into OKness and keep us there.

BECOMING A CONFIDENT BELIEVER

When I'm OK—You're OK believers walk down the street, they feel OK and think OK. Their minds seem well-balanced, their purpose clear, their attitude hopeful, open, and expectant. Beautiful things appear more beautiful. They seem able to love more genuinely (OK Child), think more clearly (OK Adult), and carry out customary duties more willingly than before (OK Parent). They not only *feel* OK more often than not, but, more importantly, they *know* they're OK. Being OK results from a decision, not merely from a whim or an impulse. For them, it is a life-stance, not only a feeling.

Becoming a Confident Believer involves learning how to change from living, thinking, and feeling NOT-OK to living, thinking, and feeling OK. This was the challenge Jesus presented to the cripple at the pool of Bethesda, who always complained about his NOT-OK life but did nothing to change it.[2]

Usually, becoming a Confident Believer is not an easy process for someone who has a strong negative self-view. Years of habitually living and operating as a NOT-OK believer may stand in the way of an exodus to a new OK outlook.

FROM PUNISHING PARENT TO OK BELIEVER

Some believers' lives may be crowded with recordings of NOT-OK Parent demands. For years, Parent may have been predominant. "You mustn't go out with those people." "You must be careful not to show any personal feelings at the party." "You have to go to church or you'll be punished by God." And so forth.

For people whose lives have been made up almost completely of prohibitions, negations, refusals, and denials, becoming OK involves learning to recognize the many positive *invitations* that surround them; it means beginning to notice the please-do messages rather than only the don't-you-dare messages. OK believers see the world as a series of challenges rather than as a set of prohibitions, a line of opportunities rather than a wall of restrictions. For Punishing Parent believers, seeing life as a series of opportunities (becoming OK) is indeed a change of outlook.

FROM REBELLIOUS CHILD TO OK BELIEVER

Some new Confident Believers may have a history of rebellious and aggressive Child behavior. Perhaps, to get their way in childhood they were accustomed to scream and throw fits, or to stomp on other children's toys, tear their clothes, or scratch and bite companions. They may have gotten angry at God for not answering their prayer for a new fire engine or resented their belief that God demanded they go to church when they preferred to play.

Perhaps as they grew older their Rebellious Child behavior became slightly more socially acceptable: bursts of anger, shouting, foot stomping, pouting, complaining, criticizing, tearing down, nourishing jealousy and envy, seeking to get back or get even or to take revenge. They may have resented church authority, the ways its laws restricted behavior, the ways it made them feel fearful and guilty. In their rebelliousness, they may have labeled the church's liturgy "boring," its theology "primitive," and its officials "socially unaware." Although outbursts may have been couched in intellectual or even technical theological language, they involved the Rebellious Child expressing NOT-OK convictions inside. Anger, resentment, fear, and hatred lodged in the Inner Core can distort the marvelous Power Within as it flows through the Child ego state and turn the energy into destructive emotional outbursts.

People who leave their Rebellious Child behind and become OK learn to allow others to feel good, to enjoy their own possessions, to do things their own way. They sometimes discover that others may have found a better technique to raise money for the church or a clearer way to explain the sacraments to third-graders. The former Rebellious Child also learns the art of cooperation and discovers that deeply satisfying inner feelings (which please the Natural Child) can arise from working together on a team. Rebellious Child converts to OKness learn to face their fellowmen, no longer with a sword, but with the olive branch of peace; they need no longer approach God with an angry battle cry, but may sing and dance lovingly and joyfully in God's presence. They need no longer view their social life and work as a series of destructive competitions, but as opportunities for cooperative growth. Rather than being preoccupied with God's possible punishment, they focus upon God's infinite love and feel free to spread and multiply his love to others.

FROM COMPLIANT CHILD TO OK BELIEVER

Other new Confident Believers may have emerged from a history of regressive and Compliant Child religious experiences: periods of sulking, hiding, shame, fear, guilt, self-demeaning, self-effacing, and so on. Perhaps they were the NOT-OK Child people who felt they deserved nothing because they were told they were worthless. In religious orders, Brothers and Sisters often compliantly speak of themselves as "last, lowest, and least."

For generations, Catholics, conditioned to think of themselves as unworthy to receive Holy Communion, avoided the Eucharist. In earlier centuries, a church law was needed to oblige people to receive Holy Communion at least once each year. And even though the legal ruling produced the desired behavior—people came to the altar rail and took the communion wafer on their tongues—the law could not bestow OKness on congregations trained for generations by clergy and parents to think of themselves as NOT-OK (as regressive and compliant NOT-OK Child believers).

Once Compliant NOT-OK Child believers enter an OK frame of mind, they see themselves as having meaning, being important, making a difference. They feel welcomed by the church, friends of God. Enjoying new importance, they now know their ideas can have an influence and that they can be a contributing part of whatever is going on. Now they discover they can think about theology themselves, without simply being told what to believe and what not to believe. They discover they can weigh ethical decisions in their own minds and need not wait until someone else tells them when to approve and when to be scandalized.

For them now, the world is open for business; there are things in society that need to be said and done, and they feel a part of the saying and doing. While before they were simply obedient—doing what they were told—they now become responsible—doing what seems best to them. Rather than never speaking and acting ("I'll just keep quiet, let others do the thinking."), Compliant Child converts to OKness are soon able to enter into the committee work or family decisions with a new confidence. While in the NOT-OK state they may have continually asked themselves, "Where have I sinned?" or "Tell me where I've done wrong." Now, as Confident Believers they allow their Creative Child to cooperate with their Adult and ask, "What can I do to create a better future?"

STAYING A CONFIDENT BELIEVER

Some people are OK believers from the start, but most people reach OKness from backgrounds of Punishing Parent, Aggressive Child, or Compliant Child. In the process they discover that learning to think and act OK is not as simple as they would wish. Biblically, becoming OK is an exodus experience; it involves leaving familiar territory in search of a new, free world.

Newly converted Confident Believers who have lived twenty or thirty years as NOT-OK Child believers can usually be driven back into NOT-OKness by a demanding spouse or a punishing pastor or by other strong Punishing Parent personalities. Or they can choose for themselves to discontinue their personal exodus to the new OK land and to return to the familiar NOT-OK fleshpots of Egypt.

As a sign of the Power Within at work, OKness is a precious commodity and needs to be protected, nourished, strengthened in every way possible. Ninety-nine compliments can boost one's spirit to the · clouds, but often a cruel word of criticism strategically placed can threaten OKness to its depths.

In the parable of the seeds and the sower, Jesus described what can happen to any group of new Confident Believers: some seeds fell on the pathway and were eaten by passing birds; some fell on rocks but died for lack of water or nourishment; others fell among thorns and were choked to death; and finally some fell on good ground and produced a harvest. The moral seems to be to let your religious OKness be planted in good ground. See that it gets plenty of nourishment (stroking).

There are strategies that can be used for *staying* a Confident Believer, strategies for learning to be at home in an OK state. These seven ways of being human seem to characterize the I'm OK—You're OK believer.

1. Sensitivity to People and Problems

As a first step in preserving OKness and growing in it, OK people are encouraged to develop the ability to recognize needs, defects, and deficiencies in the religious situations they encounter. For example, if there is a turmoil or crisis in the parish or community, Confident Believers ask, "Where does the problem seem to come from, and where does it seem to be leading?" They learn to recognize the currents and crosscurrents of a problem, to get to the source of it. One farsighted clergyman symbolically described his concern for the church:

A correct analysis of the symptoms of a disease must precede any attempt at a cure; there is no other way. A man at sea can find out where he is if he uses a compass, observes which way the wind is blowing, and takes account of the currents and crosscurrents which carry or impede his boat.

Just as sailors at sea have sextant and compass to guide them, believers have tools for analyzing religious problems. These tools are basically Adult techniques: asking questions, looking for reasons, searching for explanations, admitting what they don't know as well as what they know. Even concerning doctrinal matters—"What is sin?" "Is there a hell?" "Who is Jesus?"—they may have doubts or questions. Expressing these can enable Confident Believers to grow in self-awareness and theological understanding.

The opposing attitude, which fosters NOT-OKness (superiority, anxiety, despair), is *insensitivity* to people and problems. Insensitive people walk through life blocking new information. Like the three monkeys with eyes, ears, and mouth covered, they say, "I see no evil, I hear no evil, and I do no evil." Insensitivity implies that a believer asks no questions, keeps out of things, leaves well enough alone. "If people in Africa are forced to live inhuman lives because of hunger or political persecution, that's their problem, not mine. I'll stay here in America and mind my own business." Insensitive believers may not harm a situation, but they certainly do nothing to help it.

Another version of insensitivity to problems is characterized by a refusal to accept responsibility, sometimes colloquially described as passing the buck. For example, "My religious superiors tell me what to believe and how to feel. Since they haven't criticized our town's unfair housing practices toward minorities, I don't consider it my business." Such people tend to absolve themselves from responsibility for the needs of other people and avoid facing problem situations that could be remedied.

Confident believers are usually thinking people, on the lookout for the odd and the unusual, ready to spot a problem at its earliest signs, or to become involved in working through a crisis.

Recently, a man with wife and family struggling under crippling financial pressures went to talk to his pastor, who gave him a sermon on trust in God. When the man came out of the rectory, he realized that he had heard some comforting words about God *but received no help.* A more sensitive pastor would have tried to find out the source of the man's crisis. Was it simply financial? If so, how could he be of help? If not, could the problem be explored more deeply? And so on. As it happened, the pastor simply avoided the man's problem.

One characteristic of OK people is their freedom to put aside preoccupation with themselves, their feelings, and their needs and focus on the qualities and needs of others. Since OK people are basically self-possessed and content, they remain unthreatened by others. Because of this, they are able to confront situations, cope with problems, and make their own decisions.

More important, Confident Believers are free to recognize and explore the talents and qualities of others, without any fear of competition from them, bringing to light their special and unusual gifts, spotlighting whatever is OK about them. Not only are Confident Believers sensitive to the problems, feelings, and needs of others, but also to their positive potentialities.

2. *Finding Alternatives*

Finding alternatives involves the ability to produce a variety of ideas or possible ways of solving a problem, or responding to people. For example, Sunday school teachers are frequently challenged to find many different ways to teach religious themes to children.

Finding alternatives supports the first skill of sensitivity. Once the symptoms of a situation are clarified, Confident Believers usually begin creating a number of possible solutions: not just one, but a number of them. Because of complexity and human orneriness, one approach to a solution may not encompass the divergent beliefs and behaviors of everyone involved. Hence, finding a number of alternatives is often necessary.

For instance, recently in a parish meeting faced with the task of improving the congregation's quality of worship, most of the people there simply lamented or complained about the problem. They seemed helpless. However, before the evening was over, one creative Confident Believer generated a list of alternative helpful suggestions:

- Develop an eight-week set of sermons exploring the idea of worship.
- Create a new congregation worship handbook.
- Enlarge the choir.
- Change the schedule of church services.
- Try worshiping in smaller groups, in different locations.
- Let interested people, not only the pastor, compose prayers for services.
- Survey the city for people who have succeeded in improving church experience in their congregations.
- Revive and rejuvenate group prayer methods that seemed to work well in the past.

Not all alternatives proved useful; some were not acceptable to the people at the meeting. But because this Confident Believer brought out of his storehouse ideas new and old, the people now more than ever enjoy Sundays in their church.

The task of finding alternatives makes demands on the believer's creative imagination and counts on his personal experience and his ability to use problem-solving powers. While the NOT-OK believer may hesitate to explore beyond the images, beliefs, and ideas that have been given to him by others, the OK believer feels free to test situations, to make estimates of the effects of his suggested solutions. For example, one small-town church calls on its people's creative imagination. One Sunday out of each month the church doors are closed because the pastor and congregation are encouraged to do their own personal "good things among people" instead of coming to church.

While NOT-OK believers never bother to think of new and alternative solutions, saying, "There are people who can decide that for me," Confident Believers find this NOT-OK approach too simplistic, preferring instead to search for their own answers. OK believers usually see the importance and potential of situations and accept challenges to suggest alternate ways of growing. Instead of saying, "Just tell me what to do and I'll do it," they say, "I think I can figure out a few different approaches to this problem, and maybe one of them will work."

Today many women, feeling free and OK enough to explore religious alternatives, are convinced they can bring new life to the churches. Some of them are ordained or are seeking to be. "Nothing is stronger," said Victor Hugo, "than an idea whose time has come." Confident Believers are people in touch with ideas, who know how to put ideas to work.

3. Flexibility of Action

While the first staying-OK skill involves seeing the problem, and the second involves finding possible solutions, the third skill focuses on *doing*—flexibility.

Many believers are willing to do things only one way—"This is the way we've always done it," "I'll do it the way I was taught," or "My way is the best way," or "I won't do it unless you follow my idea." Such inflexible believers are usually driven by a Punishing Parent or a Rebellious or Compliant Child. Seldom open to doing anything in a new way, they find experimentation painful and are skeptical of innovation. "Why try a new way when we know the old way works perfectly well?"

Confident Believers develop their Free Child's eye for seeing truth in new ways, in unsuspecting places. For example, one OK believer learned to read the New Testament, sometimes viewing Jesus as a social revolutionary, sometimes as an itinerant preacher, sometimes as a healer; he learned to notice how each viewpoint of Jesus gave him new insights. He also read how others interpreted the biblical meaning of Jesus and enjoyed reflecting upon their various interpretations.

Free from the inertia of prescribed thought—the slavery mentality —Confident Believers see the richness of human experience and do not feel forced to interpret an event in one and only one way. They learn to accept people with radically different beliefs and to enrich their experience by testing new values and viewpoints.

The biblical book, the Acts of the Apostles, is a testimony to the flexibility of Jesus' apostles. In the presence of the Spirit, they discovered their new OKness, the Power Within, and couldn't wait (eagerness of the Child) to share their wonderful feelings with others. They were free enough to adopt innovative ways of preaching the good news. They organized communal living groups, formulated missionary policy, created an institutional structure for the church, wrote doctrinal letters, changed Jewish dietary regulations, and created liturgical practices in new countries to fit the customs and cultures of each place. In their confident OKness, the apostles were sensitive to problems in the new church, found alternative solutions, and carried out the solutions that seemed best for everyone.

Flexibility of action can involve doing something to bring about personal maturity and responsibility, psychological health, or the experience of fellowship; it may mean working against poverty, for racial equality, for peace, or for the rights of citizens before the law. Doing something constructive about any or all of these is a challenge to the the Confident Believer's flexibility of action.

The NOT-OK believer will be recognized by his inability to act in new and innovatively helpful ways.

4. *Originality of Response*

NOT-OK believers tend to respond in the same old way. Their behavior is usually predictable. Put them in a particular situation, and everyone knows what they will do. Even in their complaints and criticism they lack originality. Consider four NOT-OK believer complaints:

(a) Let the children memorize Bible verses; it was good enough for us, it'll be good enough for them.
(b) There's nothing you can do to get the poor out of their hole; even the Lord himself told us we'd always have them with us.
(c) Didn't I tell you those new hymn books wouldn't work? And look at all the money we wasted on them.
(d) Today's young people are a generation of fornicators; they need the fear of God shaken into them.

In contrast, Confident Believers will tend to produce uncommon responses, ones that are fresh, genuinely springing from their own thoughts and experiences. Parallel to the set of unoriginal NOT-OK responses might be the following set of rather uncommon OK responses:

(a) If the theologians say we can find God in all things, maybe the young people can learn to find him in their own music.
(b) Let's see if we can't at least start a dental clinic for the people in this slum neighborhood. We may not solve the poverty problem, but we can take one step.
(c) I asked people about the hymn books and discovered that the problem was simply a confusion between page numbers and hymn numbers.
(d) Young people today are in search of deeper levels of interpersonal relationships. Even when they do wrong, the important thing is to

nourish their growing love for each other. Wrongdoing can be transformed into a learning experience.

One pastor explained his mission in the following way: "I have
decided to use Transactional Analysis when I preach a sermon because I am convinced that becoming an OK person is the first step
to becoming an OK believer." This clergyman sees himself as a
twentieth-century Christian trying to do in today's world what a
Christian apostle was trying to do in the first century. Each of them,
twenty centuries apart, was exhibiting OK originality.

In originality, Confident Believers may produce remote or unusual
associations among things. For example, one may see ways that an
astronaut or a deep-sea fisherman can help bring about the kingdom
of God. Another may see how young people's popular music can be
used to reflect important life values. A third may discover the best
time for prayer is while cooking supper. Why not? What does it
matter if no one has ever done this before or even thought of it? It
springs out of the Power Within.

NOT-OK Parents might place strong taboos on original thinking.
"Don't go talking with that free thinker." "Don't read those sick
books by Sartre, Schonpenhauer, or Nietzsche." "We don't need
any of your Pentecostal friends here, and I don't want any child of
mine going to their meetings."

Instead of originality, the NOT-OK Child prefers imitative behavior, to do what everyone else does. Like the child in the classroom
who says, "Teacher, Jimmy is doing it the wrong way," NOT-OK
believers usually find originality upsetting, threatening, and uncom-
fortable. As long as everybody does it the same way, no one has to
think about it. No one has to decide whether it's good or bad,
helpful or unhelpful, desirable or undesirable.

For NOT-OK believers, "tradition and experience" is defined stati-
cally ("This is what our parents learned and handed on to us; we
must do exactly what they told us to."). For OK believers, "tradition
and experience" is dynamic and exciting ("Keeping in mind what
our parents learned and handed over to us, let's see how we can

carry on their work a step further."). While NOT-OK believers may be content to memorize the catechism or Bible verses, OK believers use the Bible or catechism as guidelines for further exploration in faith. Originality initiates growth.

Christian orthodoxy in general resembles a clothing store which contains enough different garments to provide, for example, a suit for the businessman, a loincloth for the aesthetic, a cap for the wanderer, and shoes for a dancer. Christian tradition contains enough different theological wardrobes to suit every personality, temperament, and way of life.

There are many pathways to God, and each Confident Believer will carve out his or her own. The Power Within wells up from the Inner Core, and each one sings the Lord's song in a new way.

5. *Penetrating Insight*

Sometimes people are called upon to deal with major problems that perhaps cannot be completely solved in a short time. Many such problems are ethical in nature: the question of war, euthanasia, homosexuality, contraception, abortion. Other questions are theological and philosophical: free will, divine grace, Eucharist, Incarnation, and many more. These problems have consumed the thought and experience of humans for thousands of years.

Because such problems often find concrete expression in people's lives, individuals frequently must make important evaluations concerning, for example, taking a political stand regarding the abortion issue, the pursuit of world peace, resolving hatred brewing in American ghettos. Other more private matters include waning personal religious convictions, the homosexuality of a son or daughter, the loneliness of a senile mother, bouts with discouragement and despair. Confident Believers accept Adult responsibility for whatever action is chosen.

NOT-OK believers often avoid penetrating the roots of such problems responsibly, choosing to defy the law or defer to it, or to find some religious authority to accept responsibility for it. "I feel I have every right to use contraceptives," said a man to a priest. "Please tell me that it's all right to use them." Another man said to his pastor, "I feel I can worship God on the golf course as well as in the Sunday service. Isn't that right?" Both men wanted the priest or pastor to accept responsibility for the decision so that they could remain the Obedient Child, merely carrying out Parent commands. While the NOT-OK Child irresponsibly looks to authority for permission to act, OK Adult believers grant their own permission, that is, they accept personal responsibility for their actions.

Confident Believers feel free to explore the deepest recesses of a problem, to adopt a searching attitude, a probing approach. When they act responsibly, consistent with their experience, they find themselves not thinking of the usual, obvious solutions. Instead they tend to penetrate the problem: researching, experiencing, clarifying, interpreting, evaluating, struggling to express the situation with all the probability or certitude the evidence can bring. "The way of faith," writes Michael Ramsey, former archbishop of Canterbury, "is not to try to bolster up old theology in old ways, nor is it to abandon theology in the quest of a kind of Godless Christianity. The way of faith is rather to go into the darkness without fearing, and in the darkness to meet again the God who judges and raises the dead."[3]

To seek insight at the deepest level of experience is to use the Adult in conjunction with the Intuitive Child. On the level of insight, an Ignatius Loyola created a set of spiritual exercises to train people to pray; a group of ecumenical people prophetically set up a religious community at Taize in southern France; a Berrigan ethically challenged the American military system by destroying draft records; a Dietrich Bonhoeffer realized that he must commit himself to the plot to assassinate Hitler. To be a Confident Believer involves finding new horizons, being in touch with the Power Within at work in people's Inner Core, individually and collectively.

6. *A Sense of Wholeness*

Confident Believers are called upon, not only to think deeply about the problems that surround them, but to translate their penetrating insights into meaningful sense on all levels of life: spelling out insights, bringing them to expression, making them concrete and useful for themselves and others.

Theologians such as Augustine, Aquinas, Luther, Calvin, and Barth sought to develop to the full their insights of God. Their writings in dogmatic theology organize their insights into meaningful unity. Although limited and colored by the social values of their times, their volumes are a testimony to the analytic and synthetic ability of the Creative Believer's mind.

Closer to ordinary experience, Confident Believer Dorothy realized that her three children were a special gift of God to her. This insight enabled her to unify her ways of being in touch with God throughout the day: when she fed or washed her children, when she bought them clothes or put them to bed, when she took them to play or told them stories, when she read about child care or talked to her husband about what happened to the children in school. She integrated her religious life and daily life as well around God's gift to her—three children and a caring husband.

Linda, sales manager in a department store, centers her religious experience around fellowship. "You are my disciples if you have love for one another," is her favorite verse in the Bible. As a Confident Believer she is able to treat as friends, not only her husband and family and the people in her church congregation, but also the sales force that works for her in the department store. For example, she encourages the salespeople to speak their minds, consults them when a decision has to be made, and often refers to herself and the salespeople as our team. She sees her friendship with all the people in her life as a way to concretize and unify her religious beliefs.

The Power Within can help build a sense of wholeness in a Confident Believer's entire life.

7. *Continual Inner Growth*

A man once remarked that though people mature in most dimensions of life, in religion many remain immature. As children grow into adults they continually transform the meanings they give to experiences of love, happiness, good food, friendship, style, quality, and so on. "When I was a child, I spoke like a child, I thought like a child, I reasoned like a child," wrote Paul to the people of Corinth; "when I became a man, I gave up childish ways."[4]

Yet many people who have matured in other dimensions of life have never taken the time and effort to mature their religious thinking. Such people may say: "God's forgiveness is the eraser that rubs away the black mark of sin on my soul" or "Lonely and waiting, God sits in the little host in the tabernacle" or "God has a plan for each person, and we must discover it and carry it out in every last detail." Without denying the vein of theological truth in these statements, they are far from mature expressions about God and religion. Such statements may satisfy a six-year-old mind, but they do not satisfy an Adult believer.

Many grown-ups reject religion when in reality they have never confronted it, for they have encountered it only in an immature form —as a sort of baby's pablum.

On the other hand, many believers do not seem to be ready for Adult religion. The apostle Paul realized that many of his converts had to be treated like babies. "I fed you with milk, not solid food; for you were not ready for it; and even yet you are not ready."[5]

One of the continual inner-growth experiences of Confident Believers is the recurrence of new insights and perceptions of reality. These in turn energize and transform the Inner Core so that the believer is in effect being reborn again and again. When Nicodemus asked Jesus about the kingdom of God, Jesus said, "Unless one is born anew, he cannot see the kingdom of God."[6] When people conclude, "I am really OK," they enjoy a sense of rebirth. Even in a "strange land," they are able to sing the Lord's song.

Whenever people are born again through the Power Within, they experience conversions into other levels of OKness to deeper levels of beliefs. These induce believers to redefine and reorganize things they see and experience. Like the blind man who sees for the first time, Confident Believers experience veil after veil being lifted away from their inner eyes.

NOT-OK people want to maintain their own mental sets, the ones they are familiar with and feel safe with. They think in the same old ways; their thinking is *reproductive* (rather than creative and productive). Usually their thinking operates along a fixed and predictable pathway, like an assembly line. For the most part, their thoughts have all been thought out before: they merely reproduce. They solve problems according to preprinted instructions. They follow the textbook and the rule. Finding it a bother to go to fresh sources, they prefer prescribed patterns of behavior. If a problem doesn't fit the instructions, they would sooner change the reality of the problem to fit the rules, rather than create new ways to solve the real problem.

OK believers are not afraid to admit mistakes or to change their minds.

The Confident Believer recognizes that the church, too, is a reality situated within history, continually developing its doctrines and dogmas. Throughout the centuries the church has modified its stand, altered its reasoning, even changed its mind. This is no more distressful than to see a child grow through reflection on its own experience. NOT-OK believers might feel threatened or upset watching their church change; OK believers see in this collective religious metamorphosis signs of life and growth.

Confident Believers realize that the church is continually developing and that it has not yet reached the level of self-understanding that still lies before it. While Confident Believers remain faithful to the church at any given stage of development, they also work for the growth and change of the church. If the church is alive, it contains potentialities which have not at the moment been actualized. The role of women in the church is a good example of this kind of development. In earlier councils of the Roman Catholics, women were systematically excluded; in the recent Vatican II Council women were permitted to watch the sessions from the galleries. In future councils there may be further changes. Change continues because of the Power Within.

Take a Moment

On a sheet of paper, draw a line in the middle from top to bottom. On the left side, list some of the words, events, or experiences that can threaten your OKness. On the right, list whatever tends to strengthen your OKness and whatever helps the Power Within flow freely through you. Are you getting plenty of nourishment to grow as a Confident Believer? What can you do to improve your situation?

7

WHAT HOUSE WOULD YOU BUILD FOR GOD?

Isa. 66:1

OK Churches

CHURCH LIFE

In one church, certain activities seem to nurture jealousy and hatred—emotions which are in conflict with professed beliefs of trust and forgiveness.

In another church, people report being hurt by an unsympathetic pastor or being bored with a stereotyped ritual and liturgy.

In still another church, people place more value on law than on love, more attention on money than on religious experience.

Still another congregation has been trained to dance puppetlike for a church official who pulls the strings.

Because of these conflicts and many other problem situations connected with church, it may be helpful to view the elements of church life in the light of Transactional Analysis.

Just as people may express themselves in predominantly Parent, Child, or Adult ways, so a church congregation may be described as predominantly Parent, Child, or Adult.

And just as individuals adopt religious life-as-a-whole positions, so a church congregation may adopt an OK or NOT-OK stance toward itself and others.

What kind of congregation would you like to be part of? What house would you build for God?

Five kinds of OK and NOT-OK church congregations can be distinguished:

Punishing and Oversolicitous Parent (NOT-OK) Church,

Nurturing Parent (OK) Church,

Hostile or Regressive Child (NOT-OK) Church,

Liberated Child (OK) Church, and

Adult (OK) Church.

Since each kind of church highlights differences in people and experiences, each will be discussed in turn.

IN A PUNISHING PARENT AND OVERSOLICITOUS (NOT-OK) CHURCH

The church building in a Punishing Parent church is a place where no one goes unless they're on business or are duty bound to appear under pain of sin or strong disapproval. Like a jail, everything in it and around it is subject to rules and regulations. And everybody knows the rules. For newcomers, the rules are posted conspicuously. Don't Touch signs leave their threats on doors, walls, cabinets, organ, altar, pews, books. To an outsider the church looks like a building never meant to be used, reminiscent of the front room of Mrs. Fussbudget's house where no one was allowed to walk on the carpet, sit on the sofa, or leave a cigarette in the ashtray. Supporting a place designed for receiving punishment and reprimands, its walls reflect generations of guilt and other NOT-OK feelings.

In such a church, at meetings, services, and other church-connected activities, there will be little or no sign of *fellowship* or friendliness. People will reluctantly participate on committees or in social events because most people—from the pastor to the sexton—want to play boss and only the most compliant will be willing to work. At meetings no one seems interested in cooperating; instead Punishing Parent expressions abound. "You can't do that." "That's never allowed here." "I'll tell you the way to behave. That's what I'm here for." "Don't ever touch that." "I don't care whose idea it is, I know better." And so on.

New parishioners soon become embittered; attendance at meetings and services grows poor and sometimes drops off entirely. People may go elsewhere for social rewards and attend other churches for more satisfying religious experience—except those who have been frightened into remaining by the pastor's clever use of worldly and other-worldly threats.

When the *clergy* in such churches manifest the Punishing Parent mentality, it will be evident in their sermons and personal dealings with their congregations. If the clergy have Oversolicitous Parents, their sermons and counsel may be peppered with a variety of rules, regulations, syrupy instructions, clichés, and platitudes. In either role, these clergy will tend to make people feel unworthy, emphasizing how inadequate or disobedient they are, displaying ecclesiastical threats and canonical punishments, playing on fears and doubts. Such clergy may assail others' lack of theological training, point out their failure to do good works, underline their lack of religious experience.

Usually the advice contains little more than unreflected-upon sayings and common prejudices. They are Archie Bunkers in clerical clothing.

Such priests or ministers may be well-intentioned, employing Punishing Parent language because it is the only method of dealing with people they know, or because generations of clergy before them have used it, or because they were taught to "do it this way." Other Constant Parent pastors simply find it easier to pick at people's faults and point out their weaknesses rather than to begin the slow work of helping others toward OKness. Often such clergy are unaware that they may be ultimately leading people away from the God they profess to serve.

One characteristic of the NOT-OK Parent clergy is that they present some of God's greatest natural gifts as if they were deadly viruses. They might downgrade, for example, leisure, laughter, the enjoyment of eating, the human body, sexual pleasure, and everything connected with "the world." They might want their parishioners to believe that the human heart is NOT-OK for "it burns with lust" and that the world is NOT-OK for its purpose is to make that lust "burst into fierce flames."

Often churches in certain areas or dioceses are cursed with *church officials* who display NOT-OK Punishing Parent tendencies. Letters to their "subjects" are filled with irrevocable orders that allow no exceptions or excuses: "Henceforth no one shall ever under any circumstances . . ." Paragraph after paragraph of "Thou shalts" and "Thou shalt nots" are laid upon the backs of clergy and people. Underlings are made to feel inadequate, insecure, ineffective, unworthy of approval. When such a church official sends a letter—which he commands to be read in every church—congregations usually groan inwardly, and people await some new restriction or limitation to be placed on their thoughts and behavior.

Punishing Parent and oversolicitous churches are sad places; they provide unhealthy experiences for even the most secure Confident Believers. At best, such churches create a situation which people are simply forced to leave or are unable to leave because of their excessive dependency. At worst, these kinds of Parent churches can breed generations of NOT-OK believers who never get to meet the infinitely loving God. Instead, a heartless vindictive God preached by a punishing Parent church is kept fictitiously alive century after century. One eccentric woman admitted that she often read the hell-fire sermons of Jonathan Edwards, an eighteenth-century divine, *"just for the terror."*

IN A NURTURING PARENT (OK) CHURCH

The Nurturing Parent *church building* breathes with a homey atmosphere. During all hours of the day and evening, people may be seen driving to and from meetings and services, conferring with each other about bake sales, confirmation classes, or next Sunday's services. People feel welcome there. Lots of activity is brewing, and things are getting done. One group may be working for peace, another working on a plan to improve schools; the church is at the center of both groups. In a typical Nurturing Parent church the major theme is *concern for the needs of people.* People there show a noticeably high degree of social awareness. It would be no surprise to discover a number of people in a Nurturing Parent church actively participating in public life or caring in some way for the community's social needs.

In a Nurturing Parent church there may be quite a few rules, but these are usually for the sake of efficient operation (not merely for the sake of rules). With people doing so many things, and equipment (tables, chairs, movie projectors, loudspeakers, etc.) being used by so many people, there is need to be well organized. While keys in a Punishing Parent church are probably locked in the safe so that no one may use them, keys in a Nurturing Parent church are most likely hung in a conspicuous place since many people use them.

Fellowship in the nurturing church, in typical Parent fashion, centers around growth and development of people. Religious and social activities are planned for everyone. Grown-ups are kept busy keeping the church socially involved; there are card parties and bazaars to run, lecture programs and premarriage discussion groups to organize, weekend retreats and conferences to attend. People encourage and compliment each other; when work needs to be done, enough volunteers always appear to carry out necessary tasks. In such a congregation, people are important and children are important. People come to church because it feels like a special home.

A Nurturing Parent *pastor* may make a Parent church an excitingly busy place where people are meeting people and many things are getting done. Nurturing priests or ministers can be recognized by the encouraging support they offer to their people. They set up helpful structures so that myriad activities can run smoothly. They get behind church organizations; at meetings they tend to compliment rather than to command. They notice when supplies are running low; at night, like good mothers and fathers, they check to see that the lights have been turned off and doors locked; they are likely to ask if anyone needs a ride or if they can make a helpful telephone call. Like a Nourishing Parent, these clergy are OK and take delight in seeing young people begin to assume responsibilities in the community, ready to compliment them if they succeed, to comfort them if they fail.

Nurturing Parent *bishops* or *church officials* will probably appear as benevolent dictators. Though letters and addresses to the churches under their direction contain directives and commands, people recognize them as coming from officials who have the congregations' best interests in mind. Regulations from Nurturing Parent church officials will tend to be protective, helpful, security-oriented, instructive. At times such officials may show a pioneering spirit, especially when they are convinced that something will be helpful to their people. And people learn to trust the experience, wisdom, and guidance of such leaders.

A Nurturing Parent church usually contains a number of Adult and OK-Child believers; this helps make the blend of people in the congregation an efficient (Parent), reasonable (Adult), and happy (Child) place. People who belong to such a church often feel blessed and are willing to work to maintain their OK community religious situation.

IN A HOSTILE OR REGRESSIVE CHILD (NOT-OK) CHURCH

In a NOT-OK Child church, atmosphere is often highly charged. The *church building* may sometimes resound with explosive emotions; at other times, sullen silence prevails. At meetings and religious services people feel NOT-OK just by being there, almost as if the place itself gave off unhealthy vibrations. When people come, they feel it, no matter who they are. It's more than the words spoken; it's the way words come out: they tumble out uncontrollably. People there are used to hurting. Such a church often lacks both the Nurturing Parent's helpful rules and the Adult's clear reasonableness. The NOT-OK Child church smolders with emotion.

Fellowship in a hostile NOT-OK Child church may seem forced and controlled. Meetings usually end up in lively arguments or sullen silence. Everyone seems to want *their* way to prevail, like a group of children each of whom wants to be the leader in a game. Little, if anything, gets done. Accusingly, people like to speak of cliques, of taking sides. "I would never join *her* committee." "Try working with him and you'll know what hell is like." "You're just like my mother." "Let's cut this meeting short so we can go out and have a drink." "We've heard enough from you already tonight." "Let me put in my two cents."

If the *clergy* reinforce NOT-OK Child churches by expressing a predominant NOT-OK Child themselves, they will frequently demand that things be done their own way—"or they won't get done at all." Such clergy must wear the chief's hat, be most popular at a social gathering, be the main speaker at every event. When NOT-OK Child clergy are provoked, they can move in either of two directions: some become aggressive or angry, throw tantrums, become argumentative or irrational; others may let their lower lips quiver, crawl away in silence, hurt to the quick, dragging their tails behind them. Such pastors can be emotionally unpredictable: on top of the world when everyone is stroking them, vicious as chained tigers when threatened, sulking for days when rejected.

As a consequence, people deal with such clergy only when necessary and may cross the street or go around the world to avoid an encounter. One parishioner might say to another, "Marge, it's safe now. You can call Father Harris. I just talked with him, and he's in a fairly good mood. At least he won't bite your head off."

Even more devastating are NOT-OK Child *bishops* or *church officials.* Their letters to people are often strongly emotional, sometimes venomous. Disobedience of subjects is taken as a personal affront. Adult-Adult dialogue is almost impossible to achieve with such officials. They frequently make decisions based purely on whim or impulse and tend to put negative interpretations on evidence. Subordinates and assistants often spend most of their day avoiding such officials. And when they must meet the church officials face to face, every other word is "Yes," "Very good," "A fine idea," "I'll do it right away." "Defer at every moment," assistants recommend to each other, "otherwise he'll give you the guillotine."

The NOT-OK Child church, whether hostile or regressive, is one of the worst situations to be in religiously, for its infection lies unconsciously deep within the emotional layers of the people involved. People who are afflicted with NOT-OK Child clergy should do everything they can to ease them out of as many involvements as possible and get them to professional therapy. Those afflicted with NOT-OK Child church officials can probably only pray, maybe confront, and, if OK themselves, love the church officials in spite of their negativism.

IN A LIBERATED CHILD (OK) CHURCH

The *church building* in a Liberated Child church allows people to feel warm and friendly. At meetings and services everything seems smilingly relaxed; there is much laughter, and people talk to each other (sometimes even during services).

Such a happy Child church may not get things done efficiently, but people seem to have a lot of fun just being together. Creative people and free spirits tend to surface in its atmosphere.

Good *fellowship* is a keynote in an OK Child church. People tend to support socializing activities—outdoor picnics, bowling teams, bus rides, dances, spaghetti suppers. The Child emphasis is on being together and having a good time. Family participation is encouraged.

If the *clergy* have an OK Child, too, they will be fun-loving and friendly. People will tend to flock around them, not to imbibe wisdom, but just to laugh and smile and be nearby. Spontaneous and sometimes whimsical, OK Child clergy exude an attractive warmth. They come to meetings full of ideas and enthusiasm, making everyone else happy they came. They may combine organization (a Nurturing Parent) with their creative ideas (Liberated Child), but don't count on it. Don't expect them always to have well-formulated plans to go with their clever ideas.

OK Child clergy prefer to enjoy dinner at your home rather than roll up their sleeves and cook for you. They probably won't get the church's annual report out on time, but nobody seems to mind because they're such nice people.

Some will probably join the bowling team and eat more pancakes than anyone else at the Benefit Breakfast. Their sermons speak of love and joy and kindness; they encourage people to become God's little children, the kind Jesus loved with a special affection. If such clergy wished, they could be accepting dinner invitations almost every night of the week.

OK Child *church officials* will show signs of warmth and affection in their letters and addresses. Rather than containing lists of directives and policy statements, their letters will usually say that things are OK in the congregations, and when read will almost sound like letters from friend to friend. Their interests and enthusiasms may lead them to start more new projects than they can ever hope to complete. But they can be depended upon to show excitement when people come with new ideas.

OK Child churches may not have a lot to show for themselves in productivity—new buildings, new educational programs, lecture series, organized census data, strong financial situation—but their atmosphere exudes good feelings and joy, a kind of promised land.

Parent and Adult people in an OK Child church will enjoy the situation best if they can put on the mind of a Child. Childlike people, on the other hand, can learn to be sensitive to the difficulties predominant Parent people might have and gently lead them into some Child expressions. Once people have a taste of OK Child experiences and realize that these are among the most satisfying religious experiences, Parent people and Adult people will eagerly come back for more.

IN AN ADULT (OK) CHURCH

In a predominantly Adult church, the *church building* usually has an atmosphere that tends to be unemotional, focused on facts, information, mutual understanding. In such a church, people will be in touch with changes happening all around them and will find changing or adapting an easy process, provided new suggestions appear reasonable and useful. When, for example, liturgical changes or new sacramental procedures are recommended, people in an Adult church will usually reflect upon the recommendations, test them, seek additional information, and so on. If the recommendations appear helpful, they'll try them. If they try them and things don't work out, they'll probably try something else. Adult believers usually introduce new ideas only if and when they decide that the changes will be beneficial to their church. Adult believers readily comply when commands are reasonable; but such believers find so-called blind obedience virtually impossible.

Fellowship in an Adult church usually nourishes an ecumenical spirit. On the whole, members of interfaith groups tend to be Adult believers. "I prefer being in a situation where I can share many different ways of thinking than to have everyone think the same" is an Adult statement. Instead of bingo parties, dances, and picnics, Adult believers will prefer lecture series, films, educational programs, editing a newspaper, ecumenical seminars, and joint social action—activities in which information and ideas are exchanged in a setting of honest inquiry and action. Individual friendships in such a church usually occur on the basis of shared interests.

Adult *clergy* will be characterized as thinking, reflective persons. In discussion, their questions will often help individuals or groups reach the heart of the problem. They are usually searching for facts and information and can apply useful information and action to situations in which help is needed.

As Adult believers, such clergy do not feel threatened by those who suggest changes in church policy or practice. Unlike Parent pastors who tend to restrict the freedom of others, Adult pastors usually point out to congregations the many kinds of freedom available in the church.

Adult clergy are usually able to see people as unique and accept them wherever they may be in the religious growth process—moving from NOT-OKness to OKness. Such clergy try to involve men and women in church activities of liturgy, government, evangelism, practical witness. Within the traditional role of the clergy as ministers of God's word and sacraments, Adult clergy start "where people are." Adult clergy learn to express their insights using words and ideas that their people can understand. Adults prefer not to confuse or overwhelm people since clear thinking underlies their very reason for being.

Adult *church officials,* like Adult clergy, are generally willing to listen, learn, and explore. Usually open to experiment, they may be first to suggest new avenues of ritual and church involvement. While they may give impetus to new approaches in liturgy, sacraments, catechetics, theology, ethics, prayer, they will at the same time maintain the objectivity of court judges in evaluating such new approaches.

While Parent church officials might view experimental regulations as a threat to Christian tradition, and Child church officials might emotionally attach themselves to such experiments as their "new baby," Adult church officials are neither too eager to quench new ideas nor too eager to have everyone accept them. For example, turning the church altar around to face the people once sounded bizarre to many Catholics; yet Adult church officials listened, experimented, and found the practice helpful.

If everyone in an Adult congregation were always acting in their Adult, such a church might appear to an outsider to be a sterile computer, a church living "by head alone." Hardly a desirable situation. However, an Adult church can create a healthy, well-balanced congregation by integrating into itself valuable qualities of Parent and Child.

In transforming any church from a NOT-OK stance to an OK one, Adult clergy and church officials are crucially essential. Change, conversion, transformation all involve Adult decisions. Once an Adult decision is made, Parent believers are needed to prepare guidelines for survival and Child believers to instill warm, enthusiastic feelings into the situation. Fully functioning churches, like fully functioning people, involve all three ego states—under Adult guidance—using the Power Within.

Characteristics of individuals involved in Parent, Child and Adult church communities are summarized in figure 7.

FIGURE 7

IDENTIFYING A CHURCH COMMUNITY

CHURCH	Church Building	Social Activity and Fellowship	Clergy, Priest, Minister, Pastor	Bishop or Other Churc Officials
PUNISHING OR OVER-SOLICITOUS PARENT (NOT-OK) CHURCH	Suffocating or syrupy atmosphere; "do" and "don't" signs everywhere; everyone knows the rules and penalties; no joyfulness	Little or no sign of it; people go elsewhere for social satisfaction	Punishing and threatening or oversolicitous in sermons and personal dealings; focused on rules, laws; prejudiced, makes people feel guilty, unimportant	Letters of command an reprimand; arbitrary ordering and punishing; makes underlings f NOT-OK
NURTURING PARENT (OK) CHURCH	Homey,' welcome atmosphere; well organized, designed to serve people's needs	Centers around growth and development of people; activities tend to fulfill personal and social needs	Encouraging, supportive of parishioners, gets behind church organizations and events; sets up helpful structures	Benevolent dictator; protective; helpful; teaching; supportive; growth-orie sometimes pioneering

HOSTILE OR REGRESSIVE CHILD (NOT-OK) CHURCH	Highly charged emotional atmosphere; people feel uneasy or afraid; tempers or sullen silence prevail	Seems forced and unfree, seldom relaxed; little enjoyment found in parish activities	Demands his own way; emotionally unpredictable; feels threatened; often explodes in anger or withdraws for days	Letters of emotional venom; suspicious; petty and jealous; demands continual stroking, but never acknowledges it
LIBERATED CHILD (OK) CHURCH	Warm and friendly atmosphere; much laughter and enthusiasm; attractive to creative and sensitive people	Receives high emphasis— especially fun and family activities; bus rides, picnics, etc.	Fun-loving; friendly; spontaneous; whimsical, creative; comes to meetings full of jokes	Strong personal warmth and affection; friendly; communicates equality among people; excitable and enthusiastic
ADULT (OK) CHURCH	Spirit of inquiry and curiosity; testing ideas; ecumenical spirit; foster mutual understanding	Emphasis on intellectual and personal development; friendships based on shared interests	Characterized by thinking and reflection, questions; not threatened by people who suggest changes	Evaluative; integrative; willing to test and try new ideas and approaches

Take a Moment

Recall three or four different churches you may have visited. How did it feel to be in each church? Was the sermon strongly Parent, Child, or Adult? Did the hymns support an OK message? How would you classify such churches in TA language?

RITUAL AND LITURGY

Certain parts of church life seem to require special attention and clarification in TA language. Ritual and liturgy is one of these.

In a *Punishing Parent church,* ritual and liturgy are usually carried out perfunctorily, dryly, unenthusiastically. Church services are attended primarily because there is a law forcing attendance. "We go to mass because the church says we're obliged to go." Clergy and people perform ritual for the sake of ritual. "This is how the book says it must be done." Little concern is shown for people's needs.

At such churches, services are marked by stereotyped formalism. Feeling little sense of community, people are not happy to be there. They frequently look at their watches hoping that the final hymn will soon begin. While attending a Punishing Parent church, people usually don't think of God or religion, but rather of the Sunday comics, an afternoon at the park, a fancy dinner—anything but the "nothing" going on in the church. Sermons, stereotyped and packed with entrenched prejudice, abound with expressions such as "God will punish you for your sins," "You are cruel and heartless people," "You should never associate with non-Christians." At Punishing Parent churches, services which were meant to communicate the gospel message, "God says you're OK," instead usually insist on the NOT-OKness of everybody, present or absent.

"If God really loved us," said a seven-year-old after a NOT-OK Parent church service, "he wouldn't let us come here."

In an *Oversolicitous Parent church,* ritual and liturgy are likely to be carried out in ways that keep people overly dependent, the pastor perhaps using platitudes to keep parishioners passive, overly optimistic, uninvolved with anything outside the church walls. In such a church, people are likely to be treated like a group of helpless children, conditioned to respond to their need for inner feelings of safety and comfort.

In an *OK Nurturing Parent church,* ritual and liturgy focus on people's needs: "People come to my church," said an OK Parent pastor, "with lots of needs—for health, for peace in their homes, with divorce problems, with delinquent children, neighborhood conflict, loss of jobs. This is what the church is for, to help people find a way of dealing with their problems." Sermons in such churches tend to be growth-oriented; they teach doctrine, encourage study, treat real problems needing to be solved. Services usually start on time; ushers are well organized; the choir, well rehearsed. If people ask for special services to meet their needs, the OK Parent church will usually provide them.

On Saturday nights in New York City, newspaper offices work till early morning to get the late Sunday edition to press. A nurturing Franciscan church in the neighborhood responded. "If the printers down the street get off work Sunday morning at 2 A.M.," said the priest, "the Catholics will want to go to mass; so we'll schedule a service at 2:30 A.M., right after work." And they did.

In a *NOT-OK Child church,* ritual and liturgical services are often experienced as painful. Services, hymns, and readings are carried out doggedly, much as prisoners on a chain gang endure hours of hard labor. Clergy in such churches might use sermon time to vent their own pet peeves, to highlight their own personal hurt (NOT-OK Child), or to spout off unreflective opinion on current new topics. No one in the church seems to pay attention to sermons or to anything else connected with the service. In a NOT-OK Child church there is little possibility for religious experience, except the kind that feeds upon guilt feelings, sin, evil, temptations, and the like.

OK Child churches provide warm and happy emotions. In fact, church services here feature good feelings: joy, thanksgiving, togetherness. Positive religious experiences are encouraged. People are able to feel religious experience. Services are designed to best help people experience religious feelings. Young people often bring their guitars and are willing to sing with full voice. Sermons are emotional and loving and encourage the same. Liturgical settings are free and friendly. No one cares whether ritual details are perfectly enacted. Sharing the time together is most important.

In *Adult churches,* religious experience or reflection upon theological material is the primary purpose of a religious service. Ritual and rubrics take second place; ritualistic behavior is merely a supportive tool. Consequently, Adult churches adapt rituals to make religious experience effective—"since that's what those who design rituals are attempting to do anyway."

In general, many churches probably need a strong dose of OK Child in their services. Though, as always, full religious expression involves a blend of OK Parent and OK Child with the Adult in charge of the recipe. Negative religious experiences happen usually because either Parent, Adult, or Child attitudes tend to predominate and block out the other two modes of expression.

SACRAMENTS

Every church has sacraments in its belief system or structure. Theologically, sacraments may be viewed as special moments of grace or divine blessing. As experiences, they are formalized events, usually involving a group of people, marking special moments of an individual's religious life in a church community. Certain sacraments —baptism, confirmation, wedding, ordination—are usually once-in-a-lifetime events. Other sacraments are repeatable, for example, Holy Communion or the Lord's Supper.

NOT-OK Parent believers treat sacraments as *requirements,* as experiences of the church that people may not partake of unless properly prepared. Hence, Punishing Parent believers with unbending accuracy will see to it that every last painful detail is ritually carried out, every last regulation observed. For them, exact and complete fulfillment of the ritual alone gives the sacrament significance. "I don't care how you feel about it," the Parent clergy may say to the engaged couple, "the law says it's to be done this way, and you'll either do it that way or you'll not get married at all."

OK Nurturing Parent believers see sacraments as *needs.* "Sacraments are experiences of the church that help Christians grow in grace and the love of God," explains an OK Parent believer. "We need them. That's why they were instituted. Without sacraments to nourish us, we would starve spiritually." In the eyes of the OK Parent, sacraments are signs of God's nurturing, protecting, and strengthening his children.

NOT-OK Child believers see sacraments as *rituals to be fulfilled.* The NOT-OK Child believer exaggerates the paperwork involved in a wedding procedure, the amount of time required in confirmation classes, the archaic words in the baptism ritual. Many young people find themselves locked into this NOT-OK Child position, especially since demands to attend Sunday school or to read the Bible may generate NOT-OK feelings.

OK Child believers see sacraments as *devotional experiences,* experiences of the church that make people feel good and religious. Baptism, first communion, confirmation, ordination, wedding—these events are emphasized as good-feeling times. They are usually surrounded by excited preparations: buying new clothes, inviting relatives, taking photographs, sharing a meal afterwards, having a party—whatever helps to intensify the positive feelings. At times, the surrounding experiences become so involved and exhausting that the sacrament itself may be forgotten in all the busyness. In such cases, in moments of reverie, the OK Child can truly savor and enjoy the event again and again, looking at photographs or movies of the sacrament, after all the stress has been forgotten.

For *Adult believers,* sacraments are *special experiences available to Christians* to use as ways of further spiritual development. The Adult can, therefore, encourage OK Child and OK Parent experiences to enrich the meaning of sacraments. In a wedding ceremony, for example, the Parent may respond to the traditional parts of the event, the Child may enjoy the deep feelings, and the Adult may respond to the Power Within as it expresses itself in this unique moment. Adult believers generally learn to use all three ego states to make sacramental experiences fully human ones.

CHURCH LAWS AND REGULATIONS

Punishing and Oversolicitous Parent believers mention church laws and regulations quite frequently. They view these primarily as duties to be carried out under the pain of punishment or as "the only way to be saved." Those who fail to conform to the letter of the law are accused of sin and threatened with excommunication, damnation, and hell fire. Upon sinners' backs are placed heavy burdens of guilt, which for some people are never completely eradicated. "Once your soul was pure white," says a Punishing Parent believer, "but now that you've sinned, even if you repent for the rest of your life, your soul will never be pure white again."

For Punishing and Oversolicitous Parents, law and ritual are the center of the church's life. The church is ruler, lawgiver, and judge. "Ours is but to listen and obey." "It's the law." From the pulpit comes the nagging repetition: "You must do this." "You can never avoid that obligation." Punishing Parents feel responsible, not only for seeing that everyone carries out the law, but are willing to inflict punishment upon others when a church command is disobeyed. In this context, an Oversolicitous Parent might say, "It'll make you happy if you tithe, and God will love you more."

Punishing and Oversolicitous Parent believers often view the Bible simply as an ethical answer book. "The gospels tell you how to behave." Such believers can find a command or a word of comfort from Jesus to fit any occasion. Moreover, they usually see only one *right way* to act in any situation. "This is the way our kind of people always do it; it's best for you to agree."

Nurturing OK Parent believers are also concerned with religious security but feel that they already have it. "Say these prayers every day, and you will discover how much God loves you." "The way to holiness is through obedience." "These laws are a very important part of our religious tradition." OK Parent believers see church laws and commandments as a necessary help to spiritual survival and growth.

While Punishing Parent believers may view laws and regulations as ways of being possessed by the church, Nurturing Parent believers tend to see laws as part of a learning process.

While Oversolicitous Parent believers may hold tenaciously to laws and traditions and are frightened at change, OK Parent believers usually view laws and traditions as the church's source of strength and life.

While some OK Parent believers may not be threatened by change, others find it difficult to adapt because they see keeping in touch with the past as a primary duty. Especially sensitive to the early foundations of the church and their meaning for today, they may say to themselves and their children, "We are carrying on valuable and important traditions."

NOT-OK Child believers respond to church laws in their usual uncontrollably negative emotional way. They tend to see every law as a thorn in their side, designed to take away their last inch of freedom, to quench their meager joy, to crack their fragile happiness. "Church regulations are a hateful burden on everyone," they say, "an inescapable cross we must carry until death."

NOT-OK Child believers may defensively and viciously strike out at any mention of change. In recent years when Roman Catholic sisters began to modify their religious garb, many felt threatened by this process and strove, sometimes out of fear, to maintain traditional religious dress. Some of these may have been NOT-OK Child believers.

OK Child believers are not very concerned with law. They are not preoccupied with it as Parent believers are, nor do they feel threatened by it as NOT-OK Child believers do. Often OK Child believers will avoid laws and regulations, sidestep them, forget them, water them down. They may even wait for someone else to point out specific obligations. "I would never have known I was responsible for that if you hadn't told me." When OK Child believers come into direct contact and open conflict with some church law, they might say, "The law is really unimportant as long as I'm kind and loving," or "God loves me anyway," or "I don't believe in laws; I believe in love." Parent believers are often nonplussed at OK Child responses to law since as Parent types they cannot conceive of anyone treating law so cavalierly.

Adult believers are concerned with laws and regulations insofar as they prove helpful to religious experience and personal growth. "Wherever two or three are gathered in God's name," Adults may say, "church laws will arise." The Adult's belief is that God is trying to help people realize that they're OK; and in order to bring this OK state about in people, laws and regulations will probably remain a part of life until the end of time.

But Adult believers also realize that laws have been changing and evolving since the beginning of religious history. Because laws are often subject to new interpretations and reformulations, Adult believers are not surprised to hear of church laws changing. They feel that church laws are meant to be looked upon with the eyes of faith as well as with the eyes of history.

Every renewal of the church can be seen as a new awareness of the Power Within. Many OK believers see renewal as God summoning his people to continual growth as they go their pilgrim way.

A summary of P-A-C attitudes toward liturgy, sacraments, and church law is given in figure 8.

Take a Moment

As though you were looking at a television screen, see yourself the last time you went to church for worship. See yourself in the pew, moving toward the altar, and so on. What kind of responses are expected of you? Do you feel you are supposed to be an obedient Child, an intelligent Child, an Adult whose opinions and responses are as valuable as those of the clergy?

At church, do you feel you are invited to grow, or do you feel hostile or withdrawn because of something said or done? Do you feel joy-filled and in touch with the Power Within?

As you see yourself leaving the church, how do the feelings you experienced there affect the rest of your daily life? Do you use the experience or deny it? Do you feel chained or free?

FIGURE 8

BELIEVERS' ATTITUDES TOWARD LITURGY, SACRAMENTS, AND
CHURCH LAW

CHURCH	Ritual and Liturgy	Sacraments	Church Law
PUNISHING OR OVERSOLICITOUS PARENT NOT-OK) CHURCH	*Stereotyped, formalistic, done out of sheer duty,* perfunctorily, unenthusiastically, solicitously	Seen as *requirements,* experiences of which Christians may not partake unless they are properly prepared	Duty and obligations are the *center of church life;* there is only one right way
NURTURING PARENT (OK) CHURCH	Well-structured, *growth and teaching oriented;* well organized; meaningful	Seen as *need-satisfying,* experiences that help Christians grow in grace and love of God	Law is *help for survival* and growth; the church knows best because of experience; continuity with tradition is church's task
HOSTILE OR REGRESSIVE CHILD NOT-OK) CHURCH	*Dogged performance* of ritual, as if it were a punishment; resistant and unresponsive to liturgy	Seen as *rituals to be fulfilled,* nonenjoyable experiences, sometimes fearful, sometimes phony	A *hateful burden,* placed on everyone, inescapable until death; keeps people immobile by fear; no one's OK
LIBERATED CHILD OK) CHURCH	*Enjoyable, emotion-filled;* seen as aids to experience religious feeling and community	Seen as *devotional experiences,* that make Christians feel good and holy	Not too concerned with law; tries to avoid it; faces it only when in open conflict; an *annoying necessity*
ADULT (OK) CHURCH	*A setting for thought and reflection;* adopts dimensions of OK Child and OK Parent approach	Seen as *community experiences* that Christians use to further their own religious development	*One important element in religious existence;* seen as evolving, having new interpretations and reformulations

8

HAVE YOU SEEN HIM WHOM MY SOUL LOVES?

Cant. 3:3

Prayer and the Experience of God

THE POWER OF LOVE

Do you know anyone who, deep down, does not want to love or be loved by another person?

Do you know any believer who does not want to love or be loved by God?

We believe love is an energy whose source is deeper than any Parent, Adult, or Child ego state. We believe that love is an experience of the Power Within calling people to respond in communion from their Inner Core.

Many individuals, families, and church congregations would like to get in touch with God's love-energy. But some don't seem to be successful.

This lack of success may in part have a psychological explanation. The problem often begins with people's personal ideas about God.

TA AND THE IDEA OF GOD

A psychologist was once told, "You don't have to go to a Buddhist temple to find someone who has a different concept of God. Just talk to the people sitting around you in your church." And it proved true when he asked, "Who is God?" to a number of people the following Sunday. Some viewed God as father, others as judge, others as spouse. Some saw God as a person with whom they could communicate; others thought of him as an inner force they could call upon for strength; others viewed God as an all-pervading spirit that accounted for whatever happens on earth. He found people had many, even conflicting, God images.

This was a very interesting situation. As a psychologist he knew that people in general often call upon others to help satisfy various needs. For example, everyone expects friends to be now jolly companions, now sympathetic listeners, now advisers, now sporting opponents, now fellow workers, now thinkers, now sounding boards for new ideas. From a psychological viewpoint, he thought, just as people need friends to play different roles, or to wear different faces and respond differently, believers psychologically probably need God to play different roles for them at different times. At one particular moment they may need a forgiving God; at another, a punishing God; at another, a loving God; at another, a merciful God. And so on.

Transactional Analysis does not question whether or not God is or can be all these things to people. Without invading the territory of philosophy or theology, TA is interested in trying to explain why believers think of God in so many different ways and how their God images help or hinder the free flow of the Power Within.

The following pages attempt to clarify how Parent, Child, and Adult characteristics may affect the ways believers view God, think about him, pray to him in private, worship him in public, and prepare for higher forms of religious experience.

THE PUNISHING PARENT BELIEVER AND THE
EXPERIENCE OF GOD

View of God. Punishing Parent believers usually see God as one who created heaven as a place of reward and hell as a place of punishment. They see God's rules and commandments, not as helps for living (as Nurturing Parents might), but as a means of testing people.

God is the authority who created the trial and who will judge each one according to the evidence: the person's thoughts, words, and deeds.

Their preoccupation with punishment, divine retribution, and justice condition Punishing Parent believers to view God as continually looking for reasons to punish people. God's eye watches a man's every action; the divine ear hears his every whisper; the omnipresent mind judges his every thought.

Many Punishing Parent believers are convinced that God is a suspicious, secret spy, intimately and vigilantly snooping into every hidden corner of a person's life.

Yet, paradoxically, in prayer, Punishing Parent believers think of God as transcendent, aloof, unreachable. They see God, not as a Power Within, but as a judge standing high above them, holding thunderbolts in one hand and the scales of justice in the other. God's face appears cold and severe to them. They might spontaneously want to describe God's face as cruel, but even to think like this would be for them a sin punishable by hell fire. They, therefore, cannot allow it of themselves or others.

Theology. For Punishing Parent believers, theological doctrines provide more ways to convict people of error, evil, and sin. Church laws create and command more duties, more obligations, more demands; the inability of people to fulfill perfectly these commands opens new gateways for meriting God's disapproval. In the light of doctrines and laws, as interpreted by Punishing Parent believers, every human response must be categorized as good or evil and will receive either divine reward or punishment.

For some Punishing Parent believers, hell represents psychologically the most important element of the entire theological scheme. As far as Punishing Parents are concerned, humanity as a whole tips the scales toward worthlessness and evil. Hell is necessary in their theology since it offers the only permanent condition that could adequately punish evil. They expect hell to be quite full of people since they feel most humans deserve to be committed there "for all eternity."

Prayer. For Punishing Parent believers, prayer experience tends to focus on people's worthlessness and their evil tendencies. Some common themes of their prayers are sin, evil, punishment, death, hell, fear, justice, obedience, and the like.

In their prayer some like to find people to blame and request that God punish such people accordingly. These usually pray *against* people rather than on their behalf. Some might even like to assign places in hell to individuals and groups of people. "Let death come upon them; let them go down to hell alive; let them go away in terror into their graves," says the psalmist, asking God to punish his enemy's wickedness.[1]

Group Worship. More often than not, for Punishing Parents, their style of prayer is rote. They tend to follow prescribed wording and procedure without deviating one iota—nor will they tolerate others modifying prayer formulae in any way. They will usually be scrupulously obedient to religious ritual and demand others to be so, too. Performance of worship and prayer will be judged severely and, if performed incorrectly, will be punished. For example, not too many decades ago, a Catholic priest who took the trouble to read the small-print introductory pages of the old Latin altar missal could have found listed there over fifty ways, by disobeying proper procedure, he as a priest could "commit mortal sin" while offering mass. These special ways of sinning against God while simultaneously worshiping him were most probably the ingenious creations of generations of Punishing Parent theologians.

Punishing Parent believers seem convinced that people are basically evil—that is, NOT-OK—and should be reminded of this continuously. Their attitude toward others is quite consistent. "Cain rules the world," wrote Leopold Szondi. "If anyone doubts it, let him read the history of the world."

PUNISHING PARENT BELIEVERS, OK OR NOT-OK

The Punishing Parent's self-view follows one of two patterns: either he sees himself as rotten to the core like all the rest of humanity— *Everybody's NOT-OK;* or he exempts himself from the overall condemnation—*I'm OK, but no else is, or I and people like me are OK but no one else is.*

Those who see themselves as rotten to the core feel they must work out their salvation in fear and trembling like all the rest of evil humanity. In their prayer they must stand before the judgment seat of God, guilty of shameful thoughts and actions, deserving punishment. Because of this NOT-OK self-view, they are forced to petition a God who is at one moment a cold, stern judge and at another moment a loving, forgiving redeemer.

The second kind of Punishing Parent believers—who say I'm OK, but everyone else is NOT-OK—exempt themselves from the general condemnation. These assume the stance of the Pharisee. For them, God still remains a punishing/rewarding God; but, like the Pharisee, they ally themselves with God, becoming themselves punisher/rewarders. Lawgivers and judges, they view themselves, like God, operating outside the law. In their prayers, "exempt" Punishing Parent believers thank God that they are not sinful men like the rest of humanity.

THE NURTURING PARENT BELIEVER AND THE EXPERIENCE OF GOD

View of God. While the Punishing Parent believer views God as one who sees human evil and seeks to punish it, the Nurturing Parent believer views God as one who sees people's needs and seeks to fill them with grace and strength. Nourishing Parent believers look to God for comfort and encouragement. They image God as a loving Father showing special concern for his people. "God would prefer to have everyone happy with him in his heaven than to condemn anyone to hell," one might say. These OK Parents pray to God as an authority figure but as a nurturing one who wants people to grow in love and holiness. Such believers can learn to get in touch with the Power Within.

Like the Punishing Parent, the Nurturing Parent connects God with church teachings, rules, religious authority, and obedience. However, there is an important difference between them. While the Punishing Parent emphasizes punishment, the Nurturing Parent stresses reward. The first tends to see people as fundamentally evil and worthless and wishes to be rid of them; the other sees people as basically good but weak and helpless and wishes to minister to their needs. While a Punishing Parent might say, "Put them in jail and let them rot there, so they won't infect us good people," a Nurturing Parent would probably say, "Give the poor sinners some love and understanding and a bit of discipline; with a little helpful authority in their lives they'll improve."

Theology. The theology of the Nurturing Parent believer tends to remain conservative and simple: behaviors are clearly labeled morally good or bad; doctrines taught by the church are to be believed without question; obedience is the overridingly important virtue— even love is formulated as a commandment to be obeyed. "A new commandment I give to you," said Jesus, speaking as a Nurturing Parent, "that you love one another."[2] They believe that without strong authority and clear rules life would be chaos; but with them, life has order and meaning, and growth in holiness becomes possible. "By this all men will know that you are my disciples, if you have love for one another."[3] Nurturing Parent believers would probably find it difficult to function in a church without clear rules and an authority to enforce them.

Prayer. The Nurturing Parents' prayers focus on personal needs and the needs of others. They see the world divided into good and evil but count on God's unconditional forgiveness and infinite love to tip the scales in favor of goodness. In their prayers, Nurturing Parents emphasize forgiveness, sorrow, contrition, mercy, gratitude, hope, confidence, and the like. They pray faithfully, usually according to prayer formulae, and they look in books for prayers that seem to resonate their own concerns: prayers that ask for strength, fidelity, endurance; those that focus on people's needs, their "special intentions"; those that encourage "good works," conversion, reformation. An example of this is the prayer of a college student.

Lord, help me find and cherish myself—to solve the problems of myself and others. Help me to respect others and to love them, to see that they are more valuable than I think they are.

Group Worship. Nurturing Parent believers as a rule enjoy group worship, especially if it is well structured. They are often found in the church pews at special services, fellowships, novenas, prayer groups, and the like. In communal prayer they usually find a mutual support for being good and doing good. "People need support," a Nurturing Parent believer might say, "and should find it in church."

PARENT BELIEVERS AND HIGHER FORMS OF PRAYER

Both OK and NOT-OK Parent believers are quite capable of extraordinary prayer experience, but in each case its tone or quality differs.

In line with their usual negative and authoritative mental set, Punishing Parents' interior prayer insights might include visions of impending destruction for mankind, transcendent experiences underlining human evil and how almost impossible it shall be for people to be redeemed.

Many samples of such doomsday prayer are recorded in the Bible. For example, in mystical vision the prophet Jeremiah saw God punishing the enemies of Israel and heard the Lord speaking vengeance upon Babylon: "Behold, I am against you, O proud one, says the

Lord God of hosts; for your day has come, the time when I will punish you."[4] The apocalyptic vision of John, too, seems at times to underline a Punishing Parent stance: "Then a mighty angel took up a stone like a great millstone and threw it into the sea, saying, 'So shall Babylon the great city be thrown down with violence, and shall be found no more.' "[5]

In contrast, contemplative imagery of Nurturing Parent believers tends to emphasize the struggle toward God, God's comforting support, and his invitation to life. Nurturing Parent insights in prayer will tend to confirm the reasonableness of authority, discipline, and rules; the importance of obedience, the fitness of structure, the necessity of responsibility and meeting the needs of people in an active way. For example, in his solemn prayer to the Father during the Last Supper, Jesus recalls his Parent responsibility to the disciples: "I have manifested your name to the men you gave me out of the world; they were yours, and you gave them to me, and they have kept your word."[6]

The Lord's Prayer is unquestionably a Nurturing Parent prayer. It is directed to parental authority ("Our Father"), stressing reverence ("Hallowed be thy name"), obedience ("Thy will be done"), petition for needs ("Give us this day . . ."), forgiveness ("Forgive us our trespasses"), strength in time of trial ("Lead us not into temptation), and protection from enemies ("Deliver us from evil").

THE NOT-OK CHILD BELIEVER AND THE EXPERIENCE OF GOD

View of God. Child believers' experience of God, like their experience of life in general, centers on inner responses. People recognize Child believers by the way they emphasize feelings. The OK Child will favor good, happy, hopeful, pleasant, satisfying emotions. The NOT-OK Child will tend to focus on negative, depressive, aggressive, unpleasant, and unsatisfying feelings.

NOT-OK Child believers often bear resentful feelings toward God, and their prayers show it. In extreme moments, their resentment toward God may flare out in anger, bitterness, and spite. They may see God always trying to make them feel NOT-OK, gnawing at their consciences, immersing them in feelings of guilt and shame, fear and rejection.

While Punishing Parent believers may direct people to hell, many NOT-OK Child believers probably live their lives there. If any group of people knows what hell must feel like, they are the NOT-OK Child believers. A Punishing Parent God has put them there, psychologically, many times.

Theology. Both kinds of NOT-OK Child believers, rebellious and compliant, desperately desire salvation. (For them salvation probably means "to *feel* OK permanently.") But at the same time they are convinced that they are NOT-OK and that God will never judge them acceptable. Conditioned to see only their inadequacies and to feel only the guilt and shame of their deeds, they need a conversion to OKness, according to TA theory, before they can ever learn to accept God's friendship and love. God says you're OK to them, but they either can't believe what he says, or they refuse to hear it.

As far as NOT-OK Child believers are concerned, God is out to get them. These believers are aware of God's immensity and of his power to affect their feelings. In their NOT-OKness they experience a need for salvation, but in their minds the Punishing God appears much stronger than the Saving God.

Prayer. Rebellious Child believers' prayers—often angry and demanding, pouting and screaming, complaining and blaming—are expressed in an emotional atmosphere. So are the prayers of Compliant Child believers, except that their emotions are suppressive rather than expressive. They compliantly focus on their helplessness, poverty, abandonment, fear, inadequacy, rejection.

A Rebellious Child might pray, "Hey, Big Man. Things are in one royal mess down here on earth. When are you going to start doing something about it, like wiping out the messmakers?"

In contrast, the Compliant Child might pray, "When I speak to you, God, you never seem to answer, and I suspect that you aren't 'out there' now and probably never were, or that you'd really like to forget about me."

While Rebellious Child believers may explode from the housetops, Compliant Child believers will probably simper in forgotten corners. The rebellious may rage against God who they believe might like to send them to hell fire; the compliant, wallowing in self-pity, feel completely forgotten by God, left behind to live in an ice-cold lonely hell.

Group Worship. Worship in groups is not enjoyed by NOT-OK Child believers. Rebellious ones either try to avoid church services or else participate very ostentatiously. Some may sing hymns louder or strike their breasts harder than anyone else, perhaps in the hope of stirring up OK feelings. Compliant Child believers may go to church hoping to feel good, but inevitably something—a phrase in a prayer, a statement from the sermon, the thought of the church itself—triggers feelings of fear, guilt, and other forms of NOT-OKness.

Such NOT-OK Child feelings are common among the clergy. Convinced that others expect them to be paragons of faith and virtue, NOT-OK Child priests and ministers may suffer long bouts with guilt, fear, unworthiness, and the rest of the NOT-OK feeling spectrum. "I had never been so horribly aware," wrote a priest, "both of my people's loneliness and mine." He saw the entire world "eaten up by boredom," Christianity in decay on all levels. "Our superiors are no longer official optimists," he wrote, describing pervasive NOT-OKness in his province. "Those who still profess the rule of hope, teach optimism only by force of habit, without believing in what they say." There is only a veneer of OKness in such clergy; beneath, they are NOT-OK Child believers. "You need only raise the mildest objection and you find them wreathed in knowing, deprecating smiles; they beg you to spare them."[7]

THE OK CHILD BELIEVER AND THE EXPERIENCE OF GOD

View of God. Among the various believers, probably the richest experiences of God are enjoyed by well-balanced believers who have a strong Free Child.

While Punishing Parent believers may view God as a judge and punisher, OK Child believers tend to see him as a friend or benevolent father "who wants to love me and be with me always."

In contrast to the Nurturing Parent's focus on people's needs and God as a support, the OK Child likes to think of God as another Free Child—"God is singing in the wind and dancing in the trees; I see his beauty and loveliness everywhere."

While NOT-OK Child believers may see in God someone who is out to get them, and their feelings include rebellion, guilt, fear, and so forth, OK Child believers tend to see in God someone who wishes to establish a loving bond with them; and their responses to him are deep and beautiful—"God wants only that I love him and he takes care of everything else."

Although the Adult believers' experience of God predictably is based on reflection and decision, the OK Child's experience tends to involve strong emotional responses—"Everything I see or touch seems divine; God is so palpably present to me, I feel him in my bones."

Prayer. The Free Child believers' prayers may be spontaneous, contemplative, ecstatic, and uncensored. When uncluttered and undistracted, their prayers often soar to ecstasy, to that experience of union with God which may be described as intimacy. The following prayer comes from an OK Child believer:

Hold my hand, Lord, and be with me while I lie under this tree and enjoy the grass and the sky and the wind. I want to feel you close to me. I want to share the joy of being in touch with the earth.

Intimacy with God, an experience that involves the Natural Child, invests the loveliness and beauty in things with holiness and sacredness.

Church sacraments offer to the OK Child further occasions of perceptible contact with the divine loving Friend.

THE OK CHILD BELIEVER AND MYSTICAL PRAYER

OK Child believers are readily open to mystical prayer experiences. For them, extraordinary prayer is characterized by an overflow of feelings such as union, joy, peace, love, and so forth. Theirs will be the loving ecstatic experience, uniquely personal, bursting the apparent limits of the body.

In ecstatic prayer experiences, persons seem to leave behind the dutiful Parent as well as the reflecting Adult and live for the moment (with Parental permission and Adult decision) totally in the free Natural Child. "Let the children come to me," said Jesus, ". . . for to such belongs the kingdom of God."[8]

Totally Child moments are rare and special in daily life, and believers are no exception in this matter. Much religious experience involves moral decisions (Parent) and theological reflection (Adult), but there are also rare and special religious moments when the OK Child has free reign. These can provide ecstatic experiences of God.

THE ADULT BELIEVER AND THE EXPERIENCE OF GOD

View of God. God has been described as one, good, beautiful, and true. In response to these divine qualities, Adult believers may desire to be interpersonally *one* with God. From a moral or ethical viewpoint, they may wish to be good as God is *good.* Aesthetically, they may approach God as the source of all *beauty.* As thinkers, they may focus on *truth* or knowledge. Theology, as a reflective science, involves many Adult activities: thinking and reasoning, collecting evidence and clarifying it, evaluating and deciding. Adult believers use these activities to light their minds' way to God. Each Adult believer's mind, led by the Power Within, seems to trace a unique pathway.

Theology. If someone offers a theological opinion different from the one an Adult believer holds, he or she is usually eager to hear it. While Parent believers might dramatically tell the someone that his beliefs are wrong, Adult believers merely see another's beliefs as different, for they enjoy exploring many modes of religious thought. They search the varied ways of God's presence and activity in the world.

Psychologically, Parent believers see religious faith primarily as a *requirement or need;* Child believers view faith primarily as an *emotional experience;* and Adult believers consider faith primarily *a reflective decision.*

Prayer. Adult prayer is built around theological thinking. Adult believers enjoy reflective reading of the Bible or other spiritual books. Religious discussions and debates help to enrich their spiritual life. Adult prayer may be described as discursive thought. Exclusively Adult religious experience tends to feature not feelings but intellectual insights—new ways of seeing and evaluating experience. While the Lord's Prayer emphasizes Parent and Child ego states, other liturgical affirmations, for example, the Apostles' Creed, offer material for Adult reflection.

For mature believers, religious experience usually includes elements of reflection (Adult), emotion (Child), and need (Parent). This is a sign that they act, not exclusively as Adult, Child, or Parent believers, but that the Inner Core blends all three ego states—as in the psalmist's prayer:

> When I consider your heavens,
> the work of your hands,
> the moon and the stars
> which you placed there,
> what is man
> that you are mindful of him,
> and the son of man
> that you care for him?[9]

THE AUTONOMOUS BELIEVER

The mature Adult believer may be described as autonomous. Characteristically, autonomous people govern themselves, determine their own destinies, take responsibility for their own actions and feelings, and throw off unhelpful and useless ways of acting.

Autonomy describes well-integrated, fully functioning, OK human beings; or, from another viewpoint, autonomous people are free to *be and become themselves.*

Though such autonomy is viewed by many as a religious and human birthright, few actually achieve it. Eric Berne explains: "Man is born free, but one of the first things he learns is to do as he is told, and he spends the rest of his life doing that."[10]

Truly autonomous people, according to Berne, demonstrate "the release or recovery of three capacities: *awareness, spontaneity,* and *intimacy.* "[11] The mature believer also learns to develop these capacities. They are signs of the Power Within flowing freely through the Inner Core.

Awareness. The process of autonomy begins with awareness. The first step in religious integration is to develop awareness, with the Adult as executive. Using their Adult, aware believers can begin to shed archaic religious ideas and opinions—layers of contamination—that distort their present perception; they can learn to view religious experience through personal encounter rather than in ways they were taught to see it. People who become aware that they act like punishing tyrants or sulky brats can decide in their Inner Core what they want to do with this behavior. They may choose to keep it, own it, and flaunt it; or they can junk it if they decide that it is worthless. For aware believers, the whole world seems fresh. They learn to get in touch with things in new ways. Berne explains: "Awareness means the capacity to see a coffeepot and hear the birds singing in one's own way, and not the way one was taught."[12]

Spontaneity, a second capacity of autonomous people, as described by Berne, means the ability to shift ego states at will. Spontaneity allows believers to use or recapture their ability to decide for themselves and to act upon their own decisions. One sign of mature religious people is the congruence between their inner ethic and outward behavior. In touch with the Power Within, they accept responsibility for their own ethical choices. Although they feel free to do their own thing, they respect fully the rights and freedom of others.

Autonomous people are usually flexible without being foolish or impulsive. Instead of following compulsions to live a predetermined religious life-style, they learn to face new situations and to explore new religious ways of thinking, feeling, and responding. According to TA, despite the influence of basic instincts or drives, despite inherited characteristics and environment, people can accept responsibility for themselves and can learn to give purpose and direction to their own capacities. This strength comes through the Inner Core.

Intimacy, the third capacity of autonomous people, involves expressing Natural Child feelings of warmth and closeness to others. In this step, believers develop the ability to love with mind and feelings, to transact with others in ways that encourage closeness. Intimacy may involve intense emotional experiences of God, a felt awareness of the belief "God is love." Many believers, not in the habit of expressing tenderness, may restrict or block their affectionate feelings.

Some believers may even feel awkward when first testing their capacity for intimacy—with others or with God. The Power Within wants to flow outward and seems to produce new and unusual responses in them. As people learn to set free their Natural Child, they grow more open to respond to others.

In summary, *awareness* allows people to be in touch with the here and now; *spontaneity* encourages them to shape their own purposes; and *intimacy* enriches their lives with warmth and tenderness. The three capacities combine to characterize the autonomous believer, one whom the soul loves.

Take a Moment

Although few people read the Bible and still fewer actually study it, many base their lives and values on what they believe is found on its pages. While all believers describe the Bible as the Word of God, many develop conflicting views of the Scriptures because of their different predominant ego states.

Compare and contrast the different ways Punishing Parent, Nurturing Parent, OK Child, NOT-OK Child, and Adult believers might interpret the Scriptures. What does each look for in the Bible?

9

WHO WILL ROLL AWAY THE STONE FOR US?

Mark 16:3

OKness and the Bible

Shirley MacLaine once asked her father if she could bring her black friend Sidney Poitier home for dinner. Her father refused to have him. "It's not that *I* wouldn't be delighted," he said. "It's the neighbors . . . I have to live here when dinner is over. You don't."

"And so Sidney Poitier never came to dinner," wrote Shirley sadly, "and Dad never reached down and grabbed the real man inside himself, because he was afraid."[1]

How many people, like Shirley MacLaine's father, are afraid to go inside themselves and get in touch with their Inner Core? Afraid to live with the life of the Power Within?

How many are afraid to roll back the stone and see what lives within them?

DOES GOD SAY, "YOU'RE OK"?

The ideas in this book and in Transactional Analysis itself are, for us, ultimately based on the belief that God loves all human beings with an unconditional love. Specifically, we have come to believe that in the Inner Core of every person God says, in effect, "You're OK."

However, many people find it difficult to look in a mirror and honestly say, "I'm OK." Instead of agreeing with God's affirmation, they seem able to recognize only faults and weaknesses, lust and envy, greed and laziness, selfishness and insensitivity, and all the rest —qualities that add up to a NOT-OK self-evaluation. Does God still accept them for what they are? Does God still speak to such people his words of loving acceptance, "You're OK"?

The answer is yes.

IN THE OLD TESTAMENT

God's unconditional love for people is well founded in the Bible. From Abraham to John the Evangelist, from the Book of Genesis to the apocalyptic Revelation, the fundamental message is that God is eternally and unconditionally loving, caring, forgiving, and accepting his people. This is his covenant with them, his testament, his promise, his oath, his will: never to desert them.[2] Throughout history in a variety of ways God sought to show more convincingly his unchangeable purpose toward mankind.[3]

The Book of Deuteronomy underlines God's merciful concern and loving presence.[4] And in Leviticus, God reasserts his solemn covenant.[5] Old Testament prophets, too, proclaimed God's message: unequivocal acceptance of his people.

"My dwelling place shall be with them," said Ezekiel, speaking for the Lord, "and I will be their God, and they shall be my people."[6]

"I will make with them an everlasting covenant," came the word of God through Jeremiah's lips, "that I will not turn away from doing good to them."[7]

"The love of Yahweh," explained the prophet Hosea, "is the cord by which God draws his people to himself."[8]

"For the mountains may depart and the hills may be removed, but my steadfast love shall not depart from you," were God's words to Isaiah, "and my covenant of peace shall not be removed."[9]

IN THE NEW TESTAMENT

The affirmation of God's perpetual and limitless love seems to ring even clearer and stronger in the New Testament.

Gospel means good news. "Jesus came into Galilee," wrote Mark, "preaching the gospel of God, and saying 'The time is fulfilled, and the kingdom of God is at hand; repent, and believe in the gospel.' "[10] Accept the good news, cried Jesus. Allow yourselves to believe that God loves you,[11] that God forgives your failures,[12] that God finds you important,[13] that God fully accepts you.[14]

Jesus' preaching centers on the divine invitation to complete loving union between God and his people.[15] The union of husband and wife is only an inadequate image of the oneness that God wants people to have with him.[16]

People are invited to be alive with the life of God, to breathe and think and love, not merely with God but in him. "That they may all be one; even as thou, Father, art in me, and I in thee, that they also may be in us."[17] This is the prayer of Jesus; he speaks it, not only on behalf of his disciples, but for all men and women who will ever hear the good news.[18]

To choose to believe the good news is to choose to be OK, for the good news announces the divine confirmation of each one's OKness.

OKNESS AND LIFE

In the biblical writings of John, the mission of Jesus is often conceived of as the bringing of life.[19] "I came that they may have life, and have it abundantly."[20] In the former covenant, God promised that the Israelites would live as his special people, his possession. In the new covenant, God's special concern extends to all of humanity.

And they are invited, not merely to be his people, but *to live with his life.* Jesus' gospel message proclaims our total oneness of life with God. God's life becomes our Power Within.[21]

SONS AND DAUGHTERS OF GOD

According to St. Paul, the loving relationship established between people and God occurs in the Spirit.[22]

"All who are led by the Spirit of God are sons of God," Paul asserts. "When we cry 'Abba! Father!' it is the Spirit himself bearing witness with our Spirit that we are children of God."[23] Within us, the Spirit affirms our OKness, helping us to realize we are truly children of God. Just as children of humans live with human life, so children of the Spirit live with divine life.[24] With such a strong bond,[25] no power can ever separate the believers from God's abiding Power Within.[26]

No one can ultimately take away the Inner Core's conviction of personal OKness that springs from God. Children of God have the seed of divine life planted in them.[27] There is no room for fear or hostility.[28] They enjoy a glorious freedom.[29]

Salvation—a term which describes God's final victory over NOT-OKness—is not something that humans dreamed up by themselves, or even asked God for. Salvation was God's idea.[30] He thought of it first. "In this is love," explains John, "not that we loved God but that he loved us and sent his Son."[31]

HIS PEOPLE INCLUDES EVERYBODY

Some may argue that God's love for his people is all well and good —for *his people.* But what about the rest of mankind? Can anybody besides Christians and Jewish people be OK?

The answer is yes. Even in Old Testament times when Israelites jealously guarded Yahweh as their special possession, the covenant remained open for outsiders. Though God specially called the Israelites, he desired that the Israelites carry his message of forgiveness and acceptance to the whole world.[32] "I will give you as a light to the nations, that my salvation may reach to the end of the earth."[33] "It shall come to pass," said the prophet Joel, "that all who call upon the name of the Lord shall be delivered."[34]

In the new covenant announced by Jesus, God desires that all men be saved.[35] "For God sent the Son into the world, not to condemn the world, but that the world might be saved through him."[36] There is no qualification on the invitation to salvation.[37] Theologically, no one can claim to be excluded from divine acceptance by arguing that God's blessings are given only to "his people." Everyone is counted among God's people.[38] The Power Within dwells in everyone's Inner Core. "All who are led by the Spirit of God are sons of God."[39]

OK CREATION

According to Paul, God pronounces You're OK, not only upon people, but on all creation. God's plan is to unite in love all things in heaven and on earth.[40] God's will is that everything in the universe—magnolia trees, Shetland ponies, American Beauty roses, German shepherd dogs, Siamese cats, and everything that breathes and grows—come to its fulfillment.[41] The creation which was declared "good" in the beginning[42] shall be impregnated by the Spirit and blossom together with God's people as a new world.

> "Shower, O heavens, from above,
>   and let the skies rain down righteousness;
> let the earth open,
>   that salvation may sprout forth."[43]

In Isaiah, salvation approaches the idea of liberation from all evil, collective as well as personal, and the acquisition of complete security. No longer will anyone or anything feel NOT-OK; all creation, permeated by the Power Within, will declare itself irrefutably OK.[44] "My salvation will be for ever," declares the Lord.[45]

THE IDEA OF EVIL

Even though people find it reassuring to think that God declares everyone OK, subtle doubts and uneasy questions occur when the question of sin and evil arises.

No matter how good and hopeful we usually feel, there are times when we realize that we have seemingly ineradicable negative forces within us. By experience we know that we are capable of overflowing with anger, lies, pride, stubbornness, cruelty.

People tend to externalize this evil streak within them. Some personify it as an evil force and give it various names; every culture has its malevolent demons. Some people locate evil in others—in the bad guys, in those who perpetrate crime and immoral behavior in the community. Still others see evil in surrounding cultural conditions or in the perverted habits of society; such conditions, they say, gave rise to war, graft, prostitution, minority persecution, and so forth.

According to depth psychology, in a very real sense evil tendencies as well as good ones are an intrinsic part of everyone. C. G. Jung called this dark force the "shadow." The shadow accounts for that in people of which they are embarrassed or ashamed. It embraces whatever is bad or destructive or chaotic within—feelings of unworthiness and confusion, NOT-OK feelings.

And so the question occurs: How can God or anyone else declare me OK when this hidden cauldron of hate, deceit, and lust is a part of me? "Wretched man that I am!" cried Paul, "Who will deliver me from this body of death? . . . I can will what is right, but I cannot do it. For I do not do the good I want, but the evil I do not want is what I do. Now if I do what I do not want, it is no longer I that do it, but sin which dwells within me."[46]

Can God accept this negative part of us?

Not only does he accept it, he transforms our Inner Core so that we may overcome it.[47] Though sin seems to be the human condition,[48] people, even while they live in the flesh, possess the Power Within which helps free them from sin and make them superior to the forces of sin and evil. The Power Within, the new life, is a treasure— precious, but still very fragile.[49] Here, according to Paul, occurs the agony and the ecstasy of God's love: Our Inner Core continually dies to NOT-OKness so that the Power Within may be manifested in our lives.[50] "His light shines in the darkness and the shadow cannot overcome that light."[51]

GOD'S SPIRIT AS A GUARANTEE

People in a sinful condition may sigh with anxiety and fear, but the sinner need only ask forgiveness.[52] God's Power Within is dispensed most readily to those who are most hopeless.[53] It is God's plan that what is mortal may be transformed into divine life. "He who has prepared us for this very thing is God."[54] God has put his stamp of approval upon us and given us his Spirit as a guarantee of his promise.[55]

Our sinfulness and evil do not hinder God from saying You're OK, for his Spirit (the Power Within) is at work in us. "God who raised Christ Jesus from the dead will also give new life to your mortal bodies through his indwelling Spirit."[56] Our Inner Core is being renewed every day.[57]

Strong and marvelous is the Power Within which may not, nor will not, be broken by sin or evil.[58]

OKNESS AND FAITH

Those who read the Scriptures closely will note that being saved depends on faith. People obtain eternal life through faith in God.[59] Is it then only to those who have faith that God says you're OK?

No. According to Paul, although only those who believe receive salvation, everyone is called to believe, to have faith, to be saved.[60]

Although faith is a gift from God and no one can command it, it is a gift offered Christ-sized by God to everyone.[61]

In each case, however, faith needs to be accepted before it is effective, just as God's affirmation You're OK must be accepted before it can take effect. Faith is always a personal free choice, as is the response to God's statement of OKness. No one, not even God, can force people to believe.

Faith, or religious belief, is not merely the intellectual acceptance of a body of truth, but a surrender in trust and confidence to God and his promises. The Bible describes faith as an orientation of life.[62] It summarizes the entire attitude of a person to God.[63] A life-as-a-whole stance, faith transforms a person's potential. "All things are possible," said Jesus, "to him who believes."[64]

Just as people can show weakness and defects in faith or grow in faith, people's sense of OKness can grow weak or become strong.[65]

To truly believe that God says you're OK is to fully accept the Power Within as a promise of personal fulfillment. This acceptance helps bring our fragmented personality into a meaningful whole and helps unify what is divided in us. It brings a new dimension to the basic realities of life.[66]

OKNESS AND NONBELIEVERS

Even though God may say you're OK to nonbelievers, can such people-without-faith ever experience OKness?

The answer is yes. OKness is experienced when the person's life is guided by the new commandment of brotherly love announced by Jesus. "By this all men will know that you are my disciples, if you have love for one another."[67]

By loving their neighbor, people, whether they know it or not, become attached to Christ. Fraternal love generates OKness, and one who is able to love his neighbor knows that he is OK. Independent of awareness of their belief in God, those who love their neighbor fulfill God's new covenant.[68] People open their Inner Core to the Power Within by fraternal love.[69] "God is love, and he who abides in love abides in God, and God abides in him."[70]

Nonbelievers can also find OKness by acting truthfully. Whoever does what is true comes to the light, and this shows that their life has its source in the Power Within.[71]

CONCLUSION

According to the Bible, then, it can be shown that everyone is called to be OK—people with faith and people without it, righteous people and sinners, the strong and the weak. Everyone is invited to accept OKness, to set free in themselves the Power Within, the Power at the Bottom of the Well, that lives deep in the Inner Core.

Who will roll away the stone?

Look, the stone is already rolled away!

NOTES

CHAPTER 1. Is There Any Word from the Lord?

1. Muriel James and Dorothy Jongeward, *Born to Win: Transactional Analysis with Gestalt Experiments,* (Reading, Mass.: Addison-Wesley, 1971), pp. 101–115, 228–231.
2. *Ibid.,* pp. 269–271
3. Muriel James, "The Use of Structural Analysis in Pastoral Counseling," *Pastoral Psychology,* October 1968, p. 13.

CHAPTER 2. Do You Know That God's Spirit Dwells in You?

1. Muriel James, *Born to Love: Transactional Analysis in the Church,* (Reading, Mass.: Addison–Wesley, 1973), pp. 181–200.
2. "That ego state in which *free cathexis* predominates is perceived as the *Self;* or, as Federn puts it, 'It is the cathexis itself which is experienced as ego feeling.' " [Eric Berne, M.D., *Transactional Analysis in Psychotherapy* (New York: Grove Press, 1961), p. 41.] Berne uses cathexis in the commonly accepted sense of "psychic energy" (p. 32). "Freud's discussion of 'psychic energy' and 'cathexis' are among his most obscure," says Berne. "The simplest course is to accept gratefully the concept of cathexis and attempt to correlate it with one's own observations" (pp. 42–43). "Such shifts in ego state, which can be readily observed in healthy people as well

as in patients, may be accounted for by using the concept of psychic energy, or cathexis, on the principle that at a given moment that ego state which cathected in a certain way will have the *executive power.*" [Eric Berne, M.D., *Transactional Analysis in Psychotherapy,* p. 38.] Although Berne here and elsewhere explained the *fact* of ego-state change, he did not explicitly account for *why changes occur* in the flow of psychic energy. The present authors postulate that changes in ego state which people self-induce may be accounted for by their Inner Core. Psychologically, the Inner Core may be described as a permanent self, independent of the three ego states, that can influence the flow of cathexis within an individual.

3. Perhaps the self-programming activity of the Inner Core in shaping and directing the personality is so obvious that people fail to recognize it. Consider a simple act such as bending back your left hand. This act, or any other, can serve as a sample of all the Inner Core's programming efforts, for obviously *this is you doing something and for a purpose.* The act itself may be brought about independent of any ego state; the part of you which channeled the necessary energy to perform the act is neither Parent nor Adult nor Child. For many, this capacity to self-program is a discovery, in that they come to realize that such an act is free and independent, like many other acts they may perform. See Edmund Jacobson, M.D., *Biology of Emotions* (Springfield, Ill.: Charles C. Thomas, 1967), p. 19.

4. See Muriel James' "Self-Reparenting: Theory and Process," *Transactional Analysis Journal,* July, 1974. In this process, the unhealthy parts of the Parent ego state are decathected. The healthy parts are maintained and nourished by the Inner Core, and a new "ideal" Parent is designed by the Adult to replace the former negative Parent characteristics.

5. Rollo May, *Power and Innocence* (New York: W. W. Norton & Co., 1972), p. 243.

6. Ibid.

7. 1 Cor. 3:16.

8. See John 7:37–38.

9. Mic. 3:8.

10. 2 Tim. 1:7.

11. See John 1:12.

12. Acts 1:8.

13. Eric Butterworth, *Life Is for Loving* (New York: Harper & Row, 1973), p. 8.

14. John 14:20.

15. Eric Berne, *Principles of Group Treatment* (New York: Oxford University Press, 1964), p. 221.

16. Alan Richardson, *A Theological Word Book of the Bible* (New York: Macmillan, 1972), p. 14.

17. Muriel James, *Born to Love* (Reading, Mass.: Addison-Wesley, 1973), p. 8.

18. Gordon Allport, *The Individual and His Religion* (New York: Macmillan, 1950).

19. Laura Huxley, *You Are Not the Target* (New York: Farrar, Straus and Giroux, 1963), p. 39.

CHAPTER 3. How Can We Believe Unless We Have Seen?

1. Matt. 18:3.

2. James Keller, *Three Minutes a Day* (North Quincy, Ma.: The Christophers, Inc., Pocket Books, Inc., 1959), 2d ser., p. xi.

3. St. Thomas More, *Utopia* (New Haven, Conn.: Yale University Press, 1965).

4. Luke 9:49 (italics ours).

5. Samuel Butler, *Further Extracts from the Note-Books,* (London: Jonathan Cape, 1934), p. 119.

CHAPTER 4. How Can a Man Be Born When He Is Old?

1. See Luke 19:1–9.

CHAPTER 5. Who Then Is a Faithful Servant of the Lord?

1. John 13:35.

2. John 17:26.

3. Matt. 23:8–11.

4. Matt. 23:3–4.

5. See Richard E. Chartier, "A Plan for Getting T. A. into Church and Community," *Transactional Analysis Bulletin* 9 (January 1970): 16.

6. See Luke 10:30–35.

CHAPTER 6. How Shall We Sing the Lord's Song in a Strange Land?

1. See Gal. 5:1.

2. See John 5:2–9.

3. Arthur Michael Ramsey and Leon Joseph Suennens, *The Future of the*

Christian Church (New York: Morehouse-Barlow, 1970), p. 41.
4. 1. Cor. 13:11.
5. 1. Cor. 3:2.
6. See John 3:3.

CHAPTER 8. Have You Seen Him Whom My Soul Loves?

1. Ps. 55:15.
2. John 13:34.
3. John 13:35.
4. Jer. 50:31.
5. Rev. 18:21.
6. See John 17:6.
7. Georges Bernanos, *The Diary of a Country Priest* (New York: Macmillan, 1962), p. 9.
8. Luke 18:16.
9. See Ps. 8:3–4.
10. Eric Berne, *Sex in Human Loving* (New York: Simon & Schuster, 1970), p. 194.
11. Eric Berne, *Games People Play* (New York: Grove Press, 1964), p. 178.
12. Ibid.

CHAPTER 9. Who Will Roll Away the Stone for Us?

1. Shirley MacLaine, *Don't Fall off the Mountain* (New York: W. W. Norton, Bantam Books, 1970), p. 159.
2. See Ps. 111:9.
3. See Heb. 6:17.
4. See Deut. 4:31.
5. See Lev. 26:42.
6. Ezek. 37:27.
7. See Jer. 32:40–41.
8. See Hos. 11:1–4.
9. Isa. 54:10.
10. Mark 1:14.
11. See Luke 13:34; 1 John 3:1, 4:7–21.
12. See Luke 15:25; Matt. 18:10–14.
13. See Matt. 6:26; Luke 12:7, 24.
14. See Matt. 9:13; Mark 10:14.
15. See John 14:3.

16. See Eph. 5:21–33.
17. John 17:21.
18. See John 17:20.
19. See John 5:24, 1:4, 6:35.
20. John 10:10.
21. See John 6:56–57.
22. See 2 Cor. 5:15; Gal. 2:20; Col. 3:3.
23. Rom. 8:14–16.
24. See Gal. 4:5; 1 John 3:10; 2 Cor. 5:17.
25. Luke 22:20; 1 Cor. 11:25.
26. See Rom. 8:35–39.
27. See 1 John 3:9; 2 Pet. 1:4.
28. See 1 John 4:7–21.
29. See Rom. 8:21 ff.
30. See 1 Thess. 5:9; 2 Thess. 2:13; 2 Tim. 1:9.
31. 1 John 4:10. See also Titus 2:11, 3:5; Eph. 2:5; 2 Pet. 3:15.
32. See Isa. 42:6.
33. Isa. 49:6.
34. Joel 2:32.
35. See John 3:16.
36. John 3:17.
37. See John 10:9; Matt. 10:20; Mark 16:16; 1 Tim. 2:4, 4:10; Rom. 11:11; Acts 28:28.
38. See Acts 13:26.
39. Rom. 8:14.
40. See Eph. 1:10.
41. See Rom. 8:21–22.
42. See Gen. 1:25.
43. Isa. 45:8.
44. See Isa. 40–66.
45. Isa. 51:6.
46. Rom. 7:24, 18–20.
47. See Heb. 2:14–15.
48. See Rom. 2:1–3:31, 5:10.
49. See 2 Cor. 4:8–9.
50. See 2 Cor. 4:11; Rom. 8:1; 1 John 5:16; Gal. 1:4.
51. See John 1:4–5.
52. See Ps. 51:16–17; Luke 18:13 ff.
53. See Pss. 12:6, 18:28, 76:10, 109:31; Job 5:15, 22:29 ff.

54. 2 Cor. 5:5.
55. See 2 Cor. 1:21–22.
56. See Rom. 8:11.
57. See 2 Cor. 4:16–17.
58. See Heb. 10:11–18; Jer. 31:34.
59. See John 3:15, 36, 20:31.
60. See 1 Tim. 2:4, 4:10.
61. See Eph. 4:7.
62. See Hab. 2:4.
63. See Exod. 14:31, 19:9; Num. 14:11; Deut. 1:32; Ps. 78:22.
64. Mark 9:23.
65. See 1 Thess. 3:10; Rom. 14:1; 2 Cor. 10:15.
66. See Henri J. M. Nouwen, *Intimacy* (Notre Dame, Ind.: Fides Publishers, 1969), p. 19.
67. John 13:35.
68. See Rom. 13:8–10; Gal. 5:13–14.
69. See 1 John 3:14 f.
70. 1 John 4:16.
71. See John 3:21.